Edward Reynolds

Edward Reynolds

"Pride of the Presbyterian Party" in Seventeenth-Century England: A Calvinist in Anglican Clothing

H. Newton Malony

WIPF & STOCK · Eugene, Oregon

EDWARD REYNOLDS
"Pride of the Presbyterian Party" in Seventeenth-Century England:
A Calvinist in Anglican Clothing

Wipf & Stock
An Imprint of Wipf and Stock Publishers
199 W. 8th Ave., Suite 3
Eugene, OR 97401

www.wipfandstock.com

PAPERBACK ISBN: 978-1-7252-5134-2
HARDCOVER ISBN: 978-1-7252-5135-9
EBOOK ISBN: 978-1-7252-5136-6

03/22/21

Contents

1

Reynolds

Student at Merton College, Oxford

"What shall we call this boy?" Bridget asked as the midwife left. In her arms, Bridget cuddled the newborn who was destined to be called the "pride of the Presbyterians" for the life he was to lead over the next seventy-six years in seventeenth-century England. "Let's name him Edward in honor of my brother, who has stood by us in the problems I have faced," her husband, Augustine Reynolds, replied.

The newly named "Edward," born in 1599—the last year in the sixteenth century—was Augustine and Bridgett's first child. Augustine was a burgess in Southampton, England that had been one of England's major seaports in its trade with Europe. However, the city was in a state of decline and the appointment of burgesses was subject to accusations of political indiscretion. Augustine and four other officers of Southampton were called before the Privy Council to answer the charge that they had released a pirate from prison. Augustine had lost his job. The family became almost destitute.

Two benefactors helped them out. One was Margaret Holmes, the widow of Thomas Holmes, who had died in 1593. She provided personal and financial support to Augustine and Bridgett even before their son, Edward, was born. At her death in 1608 she left her house and an orchard to be sold in support of Augustine's children. The other benefactor was Uncle Edward, for whom the young Edward was named.

Edward accused his brother Augustine of being "a bad brother of mine who dishonestly employed money" that should have been paid for a shipment of goods. This resulted in the goods having to be returned at cost. He said Augustine's behavior brought "special shame and grief" to him. Edward told his future wife that he wanted Augustine's situation to be kept "very secret." He felt Augustine's behavior was a serious embarrassment to the family.[1]

However, Augustine's behavior didn't change his concern to help his young namesake Edward. He recognized early that his nephew was intelligent and could profit from any assistance he might be able to give. Through his connection with Sir Henry Saville, warden of Merton, Oxford's oldest college, he was able to arrange for his nephew Edward to be admitted on a special program for students from less-well-off families. When he matriculated on January 26, 1616, young Edward was given the title of "postmaster" by the college.[2]

Oxford was an eye-opening experience for mid-adolescent Edward. For one thing, he discovered that he was very good at philosophy and biblical languages. These talents earned him a probationary fellowship when he graduated with a bachelor degree in 1618. This gave him sustenance and prestige. Then, too, he quickly realized that Oxford was very involved in the ongoing dialogue concerning the non-Catholic structure of the Church of England since Henry VIII had declared himself a replacement for the Pope less than a century earlier.

The English Reformation had begun, but very differently than it had started in the rest of Europe. Only in England did the Reformation directly result from the action of a monarch. Oxford was very against Catholic ritualism and very supportive of

1. This account of the relationship between Edward Reynolds and his uncle is noted in Jeremiah, *Edward Reynolds*, 7–9.

2. Jeremiah. *Edward Reynolds*, 9. "Postmaster" was a designation referring to residence, not to the dispersal of mail.

preaching, thinking, and personal development. The majority of professors felt Calvinism was the alternative that promoted most of these points of view. In the eleven years he spent at Merton, Reynolds became strongly convinced of this position.

Reynolds had grown up with the English king being the head of the church. Oxford professors were pleased that a male had finally assumed the throne of England in spite of the fact he was not a descendent of Henry. With the death of Elizabeth in 1603, James, son of Mary Stuart, "Mary Queen of Scots," became king. King James I had greatly pleased the English Puritans, including the Oxford Calvinists. He had been raised in Scotland, where the state church had been Presbyterian since 1560. In the first year of James's reign, the Puritans had come in force and presented the king with a "Millenary Petition" (signed by a thousand Puritans) urging him to strengthen Calvinism within the Church of England.

Believing strongly that he ruled by divine right, James met only one request of the petition—the request for a new translation of the Bible that would include a Puritan emphasis. In 1604 James had authorized this revision that was to be determined by committees and printed without footnotes. It replaced the Catholic Geneva Bible. In 1611, the so-called "King James" version of the Bible came off the press. It became world-famous. None of the revised translations since that time have replaced the King James Version in popularity. Some critics have said that it was an honor that James I neither sought nor deserved. The facts prove otherwise. He was very involved in both the design and the outcome of the new translation process.

In 1604, just over twelve months into his reign James I called a conference at Hampton Court for the single purpose of having a new translation of the Bible undertaken. Although he clearly undertook this endeavor to please the Puritans, he instructed the translators to limit the Puritan emphasis in their work. He explicitly forbade marginal notes and affirmed the bishop of London's request that there be no marginal notes. James insisted that the translation support the divine right of kings as well as the ecclesiastical structure of the Church of England. For example, James instructed the word "church" would always be used instead of "congregation" and clergy would always be described as "educated" and "ordained." The King James Version has often been lauded for its use of Elizabethan English and this was likely due to James's insistence that the translation "be familiar to readers as well as to listeners." James I was very involved, as can be seen.[3]

Forty-seven scholars were divided into committees of two for each section of the Bible and the Apocrypha. They were instructed to use the Bishops' Bible as the standard and the biblical languages of Hebrew, Aramaic, Latin, and Greek as needed. All translators were Church of England clerics save one. Without doubt, it was the most highly organized set of scholars ever assembled in an undertaken translation. They completed their work in 1608 and it was reviewed by a committee in 1609. None of the translators were paid directly for their work, but the king sent a letter to Archbishop Bancroft instructing him to publicize a personal request to all citizens to encourage their bishops to appoint these translators to pastoral appointments at churches who could pay them worthy salaries. Once again, King James I illustrates his investment and involvement.

Unfortunately, the fame of this translation had little effect on the dialogue about church order that was to follow. Nevertheless, Edward Reynolds became a Royalist Presbyterian at Oxford and remained so the rest of his life, including those final years during which he served as the Anglo-Catholic Church of England Bishop of Norwich. There is little evidence that anti-Calvinism made any inroads at Merton during the first quarter of the seventeenth century. The only public opposition came from the challenge of Arminianism—a pro-Catholic, ritualistic, anti-predestination, pro-free-will point of view.

The single evidence that Reynolds had not been swayed to change his opinions came in a sermon he preached during a Calvin-Arminius controversy that arouse between Peter Heyln, a candidate for the BD, and Professor John Prideaux, long-time Professor of Divinity at Merton who was an advocate of predestination,

3. The article from Wikipedia on the "King James Bible" details this process.

election and the decrees of God. In August of 1927, Reynolds, preaching in the Merton Chapel, strongly defended his old professor, Prideaux, against the young Arminian degree candidate. Unfortunately, we do not have a copy of that sermon.

The year 1627 was some some time after Reynolds himself had been ordained and we see in this sermon a habit that characterized the format of his responses to events and issues throughout his lifetime. Reynolds became a well-known preacher and published many of his sermons in books. By 1927 he had already published one book of sermons.

This difference of conviction over predestination was imbedded in a larger issue: the doctrine of God. The theologian John Calvin, and those who affirmed his teachings, asserted the absolute power of God to determine the destiny of human beings quite apart from any freedom of choice or rejection of God's decision. The theologian Jacob Arminius, and others who agreed with him, asserted God created humans in his image with the ability to choose to follow his will for their lives. In seventeenth-century England, Calvin was represented by the Puritans and Presbyterians while Arminius was represented by the Anglo-Catholics and Church of England traditionalists. Ironically, the Calvinist's preference for church order emphasized preaching that was based on a well-thought-out psychology of conversion while the Arminiusts emphasized rituals that implicitly assumed affirmation rather new choice. One would think that, since the choice for God would have been predetermined, Calvinistic church order would emphasize acceptance of God's decision rather than a choice to convert. Further, where Arminius had full sway, one would expect little emphasis on evangelism and conversion. Irony seems to be the rule.

However, Reynolds remained pro-Calvin and anti-Arminian throughout his lifetime. Nevertheless, he became known as a "Moderate Presbyterian" in that he was always willing to tolerate and accommodate other points of view and was never known as strident or radical in stating his opinions. This was especially obvious when, toward the end of his life, he was among the very few

Calvinists who accepted an invitation to be a bishop within the pro-Catholic format of the Church of England. He allowed much freedom of ministry within the churches under his supervision.

2

Reynolds Is Ordained and Gets Married

IN 1618 REYNOLDS RECEIVED his BA from Merton and moved across the street as a Probationary Fellow—a promotion because of his mastery of Greek. He became a Fellow in 1619 and remained at Oxford until 1627. It was during these years that he spent much time in reflection, becoming rooted in his own person. He transferred to Cambridge and got an MA in preparation for ordination. He was now ready to commit himself to the ministry of the church. He took Holy Orders and wrote a thesis titled *Meditations on the Holy Sacrament of the Lord's Last Supper*. This became his first published work in 1638.[1] Reynolds stated these meditations were written "with respect only to mine own private use many years since I have been emboldened to present this small essay into the hands of so greatly learned, eloquent, and judicious a person as Sir Henry Marten [to whom he dedicated this thesis] when I was a young Student in the University, as my first Theological Essay." As was typical of all his sermons that were to follow, this sermon had both a spiritual and an ethical application.

Shortly after his ordination into the priesthood of the Church of England in 1627, Reynolds surprised everyone by resigning his

---

1. Benedict and Reynolds, *Whole Works of the Right Rev. Edward Reynolds* does not include this meditation.

Merton fellowship in order to marry. Theretofore he had been observed to be a quiet and serious student. One has to assume there was some interaction between fellows of the colleges, but Reynolds did not seem to stand out as being interested in social contact outside his studies. However, there was a social occasion at Magdalen College to which all fellows were urged to attend. John Harding, the former president of Magdalen, was retiring and this party was held in his honor. Harding's sixteen-year-old daughter, Mary, was helping to host the event. She was pretty and vivacious. Her evident intelligence was conveyed in her laughter at the comments of the somewhat older fellows. Edward Reynolds felt emotions that were usually foreign to him.

Soon after the event at Magdalen, Reynolds set out to follow the formal protocols of the day by which a young man asked a girl's father for her hand in marriage. Reynolds's reputation as an outstanding scholar and a serious, religious person no doubt made President Harding think positively about Reynolds's request. Although at age twenty-eight, he was older than average, Reynolds's achievements made him very desirable. Immediately, Reynolds contacted his uncle Edward to assist him in making the financial and social arrangements.

A series of distinct steps determined marriage arrangements in mid-seventeenth-century England for persons in the professions.[2] The first was a written legal contract between the parents concerning marriage arrangements. Uncle Edward took the place of his family in negotiations of Reynolds's side in this step.

The second step was a formal exchange before witnesses of oral promises to each other. Both Edward and Mary were quite willing to commit themselves to each other. This was followed by three public proclamations of banns (vocal announcements) that the marriage was to take place. The fourth step was the actual wedding in church when mutual consent and commitment were stated and verified. Here the church gives its blessing to the marriage. The last step was sexual consummation. All these steps except the last were public to one degree or another. Later in the century, the

---

2. Jeremiah details these steps in *Edward Reynolds*, 52–55.

Puritans/Presbyterians added to the reasons for marriage "mutual support in prosperity and adversity, the avoidance of fornication as well as procreation and the care of children."[3]

Mary and Edward solved the problem of financial support by Reynolds accepting a vacant appointment as vicar of All Saints Church in Northampton. This city was Mary's hometown, which she knew well.

Reynolds was fairly inexperienced in the ways of sexual relationships. Fortunately for Edward, his bride was not so inhibited. Mary was well-versed in the knowledge of sexual consummation as the final step of marriage. Many young women were already married in their teens and were very willing to share their knowledge of these new experiences with their girlfriends. Mary was bright, sensitive, and extroverted, and eager to share her knowledge with her older and less worldly-wise husband. They had a long and good marriage. They had three children—one son, Edward, and two daughters, Mary and Elizabeth.

Their time at All Saints, Northampton was a comfortable place to begin their marriage and ministry. Before a year had passed, however, Edward was called to a prestigious ministry he could not turn down. He was invited to become the reader (preacher) of divinity at Lincoln's Inn in London. The well-known John Donne had resigned this post to become Dean of St. Paul's Cathedral in London in 1621. John Preston, a young and controversial preacher, replaced Donne. Preston died on July 20, 1628 shortly before he was forty-one years old, and this left the position open.

Reynolds's reputation had already grown enough for him to be recognized as the ideal person for this job of preaching to young law students. It was a very significant post. The Society of Lincoln's Inn was an organization that maintained attorney's chamber and offices for those preparing for and serving as lawyers. It had originally been within the city limits of London but King Henry I had decided that no such institute of legal training should exist in the city and the Pope had decreed that clergy should teach only canon, but not common, law. The Society of Lincoln's Inn moved

3. Jeremiah, *Edward Reynolds*, 55.

to Holborn just outside London's city limits. The reader in Divinity was established for clergy to preach to future lawyers. In 1631 three sermons he had delivered at Lincoln's Inn were published as *Three Treatises of the Vanity of the Creature, the Sinfulness of Sin, and the Life of Christ, Being the Substance of Several Sermons Prepared and Delivered at Lincoln's Inn.*[4]

However, in spite of the value that Lincoln's Inn was for Reynold's career advancement, this assignment took him away from his wife and family. Furthermore, he also missed being in a parish of people where he would have the leisure to study and write. He accepted the appointment to Braunston—a village situated on a hill at the junction of two canals with a windmill that could be seen from far away. Reynolds felt at home where boats on the canals completed a pastoral picture. On March 1, 1631, he resigned his position at Lincoln's Inn and became the rector at Brauston, Morthhamptonshire where he remained for the next thirty years. Brauston became the hub of much of his development as the widely published preacher and advocate of Presbyterianism.

---

4. These are included in Benedict and Reynolds, *Whole Works of the Right Rev. Edward Reynolds*, 1–475.

3

Reynolds Writes a Book

WE KNOW LITTLE OF Edward Reynolds's private life in college. Moreover, we know even less about his life as a boy or young man. We can only guess he knew a little bit about his father's difficulties and the fact that some lady had given money and a house to the family. Further, he was obviously aware he had the same name as his uncle and that this uncle had always shown special interest in him. The family appears to be nonreligious. Nevertheless, Edward Reynolds's life leading up to his matriculation at Merton College seems to have been fairly typical for middle-class youth in early seventeenth-century England. These were the fairly mundane, peaceful early years of the reign of James I, the son of Mary Queen of Scots. When Reynolds left for college, the Bible he would study had become the new translation authorized by his king—the translation that would soon become known as the King James Version.

What vocation Edward Reynolds had in mind, if any, during his early Oxford education is unclear. A typical Oxford curriculum has always been—from that day to this—extensive study of history, philosophy, languages. Reynolds excelled in the mastery of classical languages and philosophy. Cambridge and Oxford were known as the institutions where clergy were trained, but that training usually followed the basic bachelor degree as a foundation. Some occasion or event led Reynolds decision to seek ordination. At this point we are introduced to a singular personal event in his religious training—he wrote a book. He had become very well-versed in the thinking of Plato and Aristotle, as well as other ancient writers who had a great deal to say about the nature of human beings. These teachings had profoundly influenced Reynolds's own understanding. His book is a testimony to this learning.

Very few people write a book during their training to be religious ministers.. But Edward Reynolds did. It's title was *A Treatise of the Passions and Faculties of the Soul of Man.*[1] This was not a bestseller—to say the least! Nor was it intended to be. In fact, this young student at Merton College, Oxford never intended his book to be published at all. He claimed he wrote it to and for himself.

Although we know practically nothing about Reynolds's previous religious experiences, his treatise clearly indicates something had happened. He had become personally religious and he had decided to seek ordination as a priest in the Church of England. He states that he wrote the volume to become more aware of himself. As he noted in his introduction, "that I long since have taken boldness in the minority of my studies to write this ensuing Treatise: that before I adventured on the endeavor of knowing other things, I might first try whether I know myself. Least I should justly incur the censure of former philosophers upon grammarians. That they were better acquainted with the evils of Ulysses than with their own."[2]

Most clergy today would react knowingly to such a motivation as very essential to the pastoral task. They would be amazed that a religious applicant in the seventeenth century would have such insight.

One might predict that if an analysis were done of those students who wrote a book while still in college, the number would be less than the fingers of the right hand; and that among those books written by students during college, the number that wrote a book of five hundred pages in length, as was Reynolds's, might be zero.

1. Reynolds, *Treatise of the Passions and Faculties.*
2. Reynolds, *Treatise of the Passions and Faculties.*

Reynolds's book has a personal history that makes sense of this rare phenomena. This includes Reynolds's own religious experience. He could have been influenced by some preaching—as his view of church order would recommend. Later in his life he wrote extensively about the nature of religious experience.[3] It could have been grounded in his own personal history.

The "passions" about which Reynolds wrote were the seventeenth-century word for "emotions." He assumed they were both the cause for, as well as reactions to, life events. The *Treatise* includes 550 pages divided into chapters that cover the functions and corruptions of most, if not all, the emotions experienced by human beings then and now. These include

- memory,
- love,
- hatred,
- desire,
- joy,
- sorrow,
- hope,
- boldness,
- fear,
- anger,
- understanding,
- immortality, and
- will.

As far as we know, Reynolds knew nothing of Descartes, who became the well-known purveyor of the view that emotions had little or nothing to do with the basic human ability to reason and

---

3. For a complete description of the conversion process see Jeremiah, *Edward Reynolds*, 79–91.

determine behavior.[4] Interestingly enough, Descartes was pressured to write his own book on the passions some time later by one of his friends who had read Reynolds's *Treatise*.

Princess Elizabeth of Bohemia was this friend of Descartes who encouraged him to write a statement on "the passions" (i.e., emotions) She read Descartes's philosophy of objectivism and was very impressed. Known as one of the best informed women in Europe in the seventeenth century, she began a personal correspondence with Descartes that developed into deep, even intimate, friendship.[5] She was also a Christian who came to feel that Descartes's reasoning didn't seem to include a personal God. She expressed her opinion to another friend who somehow knew of an Oxford student who had written a book of reflections on human experience that did include Christian reasoning. This book was none other than Reynolds's *Treatise*, which lay unpublished among his papers on the shelf of Oxford's Bodelin Library. It is unclear who Reynolds's friend was that knew he had written the *Treatise*. Somehow, Princess Elisabeth obtained a copy and was very impressed by what she read. Reynolds knew nothing of this. He did not know she had obtained a copy and read it.

By the time this happened, several years had passed. Reynolds was already ordained, married, a priest in a church, and the author of several sermons that were already published.[6] He had not even thought about the *Treatise* for a long time. Princess Elizabeth made contact with Reynolds and complimented him. She was very impressed with Reynolds's book and wondered why he had never published it. She strongly recommended that he do so.

He had two different reactions. The first was excitement. He had never considered it for publication before. He was honored to be sought out by a princess. She was attractive and seductive. He was married and did not know how his wife would react. She had not known of the *Treatise* before. The second was hesitance and

---

4. Descartes, *Discourse on the Method of Rightly Conducting One's Reason*.

5. Chapiro, *Correspondence between Princess Elizabeth of Bohemia and Rene Descartes*.

6. Benedict and Reynolds, *Whole Works of the Right Rev. Edward Reynolds*.

fear. He was already gaining a reputation as spokesman for Presbyterian convictions and Biblical insight. Such a publication as the *Treatise* might be perceived as a non-biblical, secular, philosophical essay. That was, indeed, true. He had written the *Treatise* early in his ordination studies and depended very heavily on his secular, philosophical studies. He decided to follow Princess Elizabeth's recommendation and dedicated the published volume to her. He also revised the *Treatise* a bit by including many more biblical and theological references. His relationship with Princess Elizabeth never went between postal mail.

She, in turn, made Reynolds's *Treatise* available to Descartes. Descartes and Princess Elizabeth were two brilliant, lonely people who believed that the other was the only person who really understood her/him. She urged Descartes to add the "passions" to his own reasoning, and Descartes published a volume on the topic shortly thereafter called *The Passions of the Soul.* Unfortunately, he died without ever seeing the printed copy.[7]

Reynolds's *Treatise* came off the press in 1640 and went through several printings. It became widely known. Oxford included it as required reading later in the century. Later scholars have judged Reynolds's *Treatise* as a precursor to cognitive psychology. The content remains as quite exceptional for a young man in his 20s who had never lived in the adult world. Recently, a synopsis of the content of the *Treatise* has been published under the title *An Old but Very Modern Manual of Mental Health.*[8]

---

7. Descartes, *Treatise of Man.*
8. Reynolds, *Old but Very Modern Manual of Mental Health.*

4

Charles Becomes King;
Laud Becomes Archbishop

JAMES WAS KING FROM 1603–25. Although the production of the King James Version of the Bible was said to be an honor that James "neither deserved no intended," that is a bit of an exaggeration because he did undertake that project as an intentional support of the Puritan request for a readable Bible free of Catholic footnotes. There is no doubt that the king set up a process that included major scholars who engaged in a dialogue with one another. This process resulted in a manuscript that has stood the test of time and, in addition, is written in the best of Elizabethan literary style. It's import can be conceived as expressing the best of the European Reformation that emphasized Scripture reading and personal development.[1]

One observer, Sir Anthony Weldon, called James "the wisest fool in Christendom."[2] He was, indeed, a serious and thoughtful monarch. Strongly committed to peace, he avoided the Thirty Years' War (1618–48). He tried but failed to prevent the rise of hawkish elements in the English Parliament who wanted to go to war with Spain. He lent continued support to the "Golden Age of

1. "King James Version."
2. "King James I."

Elizabethan literature" with such writers as William Shakespeare, John Donne, Ben Jonson, and Sir Francis Bacon writing during his reign. He himself was author of *Daemonologie*; *The True Law of Free Monarchies*; and *Basilikon Doron*.

James was succeeded on the throne of England, Scotland, and Ireland by Charles I, who inherited the throne after the death of his brother Henry in 1612. Charles married the Bourbon princess Henrietta Maria of France in 1625. She was Roman Catholic—a background that was to influence events in the days to come.[3] Charles believed strongly in the divine right of kings and was determined to rule according to his own conscience without consulting Parliament. Many persons opposed his policies. He was perceived an absolute, bombastic ruler. He assessed taxes without the support of Parliament, among other unilateral decisions. The Puritans and Scottish Covenanters thought his religious policies too Catholic—which they turned out to be.

He supported the Anglo-Catholics in the Church of England by appointing William Laud as Archbishop of Canterbury. He was definitely pro-Catholic in his decisions. He attempted to force the Church of Scotland, which was Presbyterian, to adopt Anglican practices. These included bowing at the name of Jesus, having a communion rail for kneeling, locating the communion table along the east wall, and using incense and candles. Their resistance prompted the Bishop Wars. He was defeated and his ultimate downfall was sealed.[4] From 1642, Charles fought the armies of the Scottish and British Parliaments in the "English Civil War."

King Charles I's unilateral, self-destructive, ultimately tragic efforts to rule without the collaborative insights of his subjects resulted in an attempt to function by decree for eleven years. He only summoned a Parliament in 1640 because he had given out of money to fight the Bishops War with Scotland. The Parliament got the name "Long" because when the king called it into session, it immediately passed an act that stipulated it could only be

---

3. Whitaker, *Royal Passion*. Interestingly, marital discord did not mean disagreement on Catholicism.

4. Wikipedia fairly evaluates this controversial archbishop: "William Laud."

dissolved by agreement of the members, which did not happen until March 16, 1660!

During this whole escapade, Reynolds was preaching sermons of moderation, tolerance, and forbearance. As early as 1641 he tried to pour balm on the growing problems between the king and Parliament. In *Eugenia's Tears for the Great Brittaynes Distractions*, he defined the true meaning of Puritanism.[5] Those called Puritans who condemned the present church and state and meant to overthrow orthodox doctrine and discipline were not to be trusted. On the other hand, Reynolds declared, "let not any think . . . that it is my intent here to insult the truly Religious and well-meaning Christian, or to brand any honest man with the name of Puritan." He wrote: "such Puritans we must be which means to see Heaven." He acknowledged the problems caused by Laud and the threat from the needless ceremonies that had crept into the church. He expressed concern over uneducated clergy who did not have the background to share the gospel without training. He concluded his rosy picture of the status quo by recommending everyone should be careful to give support to their prince or government.[6]

By July 1642, Reynolds was less sanguine about the situation in the country than he had been. He addressed the House of Commons in St. Margaret's Church. He spoke to each citizen's individual sin and the sin of the nation as a whole in a sermon titled "Israel's Petition in Time of Trouble." He stated: "I looked upon you in your double Relation, both common as Christians and special as men entrusted with the managing of those arduous and most pressing difficulties under which the distempered Kingdom is now groaning."

The published version of this sermon continues: "I have therefore presented a new Petition [among the many that had been presented to the government] dictated and drawn up to our hands by God's own Spirit, unto which both King and Parliament, Peers,

---

5. Reprinted in Benedict and Reynolds, *Whole Works of the Right Rev. Edward Reynolds*. Pagination unclear.

6. Reprinted in Benedict and Reynolds, *Whole Works of the Right Rev. Edward Reynolds*. Pagination unclear.

and Prophets, and People must all subscribe, and with prostrate and penitent hearts unto him, who stand in the Congregation of the mighty and judges amongst the gods, that he would take away all our iniquity, and receive us into favor again, and accept a Covenant of new obedience." His text was Hosea 14:2: "Take with you word, and return to the Lord, say unto him, Take away all iniquity and receive us graciously." He finished with this comment: "I must read my text, 'O Israel,' yet I must apply 'O England' . . . I shall therefore humbly offer a double Exhortation unto all of you. First that every one of you would seriously endeavor to take away all iniquity from his person . . . Secondly, As you must take away sin from your selves, so make it your principal work to take away iniquity out of the land."[7]

Charles's destiny went from bad to worse. He was defeated in 1645 by a Scottish force. He refused to accept a constitutional monarchy that would govern with Parliament, choosing to ignore it instead. He escaped his captors but was recaptured and sent to the Isle of Wright. He was then tried before a portion of the "Rump" Parliament. King Charles I was convicted and executed for high treason before a few thousand spectators in London in January 1649.[8]

Reynolds was troubled that the state would take such action against one who ruled by divine right.

7. Benedict and Reynolds, *Whole Works of the Right Rev. Edward Reynolds*, 38–39.

8. Robertson, *Tyrannicide Brief*.

5

Reynolds as Evangelical Preacher

REYNOLDS EMPHASIZED THE TASK of preaching in his understanding of the role of the minister. In his later role as Bishop of Norwich he clarified preaching as teaching and saw this as the main task of parish minister. It is interesting that nowhere does Reynolds deal with the minister's pastoral role in times of sickness, death, or routine administration of rituals. This last kind of worship, ritualism, he considered Catholic in that it did not challenge persons as to whether they had a need for personal conversion and faith development.[1] This kind of ritualistic observance Reynolds saw as secondary to the primary task of preaching for conversion toward faith development.[2]

Reynold's convictions about conversion and faith development go significantly beyond a simple personal preference for preaching over ritual worship. He grounds his convictions in a very thoughtful psychological theory of what goes on within human beings when they become Christian believers. The reasoning that exists in Reynolds's *Treatise* (written before he was ordained),

1. McCullough et al., *Oxford Handbook of the Early Modern Sermon*. See chapter 20 of this book, "Preaching and Parliament, 1640–659" by Tom Webster, esp. the following quote: "It would be a category error to divide to divide 'religion' and 'politics' in the early modern sermon" (404).

2. Jeremiah, *Edward Reynolds*, x–xi.

coupled with his reflections since his preaching experience, re-sulted in a multi-faceted analysis of the several processes that take place within individuals as they become believers and grow in their Christian faiths.[3]

Reynolds considered his analysis of conversion to be grounded in the dual theological covenants of both grace and work (God's gift of gracious acceptance in Christ and the gift of God's call for humans to engage in loving action). The European Reformation had been largely focused on the covenant of grace. Reynolds stated that in creation God entered into a covenant with man to join him in having dominion over all of God's earth through love. Adam had violated God's intention and incurred God's judgment by his willful behavior. It is important to note that this violation was self-conscious and intentional. It was an act of the mind. This is the nature of sin. It is strategic to remember this because of Reynolds's claim that faith is, also, an intelligent act.

Humans do not have sufficient knowledge to save themselves although they retain some "shadows of religious knowledge." This results in the possibility of moral acts even though the heart and mind are darkened as to the true nature of this behavior—which lies in an understanding of its meaning within the covenant of works. Reynolds implies that, even after the fall, the law (God's will for life) written in the heart of man is still a source of salvation. This provides the foundation for humans to receive a new covenant experience— seen in embracing faith in the Lord Jesus Christ.

This provides Reynolds a basis for claiming that conversion is an intellectual experience. Herein lies his psychology of Christian experience. In his sermon on the life of Christ, Reynolds notes five ways that the violation of the will of God in creation (the law) could be resolved:

1. It could be obeyed (although it was not—before or after),

2. It could be corrected by God in humans (by God showing mercy and grace—which he had not done before Christ),

---

3. Jeremiah, *Edward Reynolds*, 56–64. Reynolds' reflections have been considered to be a significant precursor to faculty/cognitive psychology.

3. It could be extinguished (God's will would not allow this)

4. It could be ignored (God cannot just do this)

5. It could be guaranteed by God's action which is available (the Grace of God believed and experienced by faith in Jesus Christ).

"Conscience" in humans remembered divine revelation and knew there was a God "to be desired." This produced a continued conflict in this conscience of fallen persons called the "natural conscience" which has disrupted the soul. This results in an "irksome state"—wanting nothing to do with God. The overriding desire is to be "safe and quiet." Sin had drawn persons into a combat from which there is no natural hope of victory. This is a "spirit of bondage." Then, the conscience "vexed" the unbeliever to review his life without Christ. "Following the dictum that the inferior faculties (such as love, hatred, joy, sorrow, boldness and anger) were led by the superior ones, Reynolds subordinated man's passions to the "government" of the understanding and the will."[4]

The Mind is, therefore, the entry point of God's saving work in humans. Before faith is possible persons need to be instructed because learning makes them Christians. One can see in this conviction of Reynolds why preaching is so vital. It is the means why which the mind is confronted and awakened to the truth of God's revelation in Jesus Christ. Faith is defined as an "assent" to this central truth. Reynolds contends that this "assent" is created by the Word and the Spirit. Faith is an act of knowledge focused on Christ and embedded in the certainty of the infallible authority and word of God. Once persons know this in a spiritual manner they have to believe it.

Knowing the truth involved a twofold illumination of the mind. One is theoretical and can be stated. The other is experimental and is practical. The mind becomes convinced by a special work of God's grace in removing from the mind all natural ignorance or prejudice that might stand in the way of spiritual truth.

---

4. This quote is from Jeremiah, "Edward Reynolds (1599–1676)," 59.

Reynolds's theory did not just end with this work of grace because the mind rules man's soul through the will. The will is a free agent in that it is indifferent to whatever is happening. It is also blind because to function the will needs the assistance of an "informing power." All of the actions of the will presuppose a guiding act from the intellect. This power of the intellect is not compelling or constraining. The will is not completely subordinated to the understanding. This explains why enlightened people sometimes commit acts they know are wrong.

Reynolds is convinced that when persons' minds have been opened to the glory of spiritual truth, "God also frames and fashions the will to accept, embrace and love those good things of which the mind is thus prepossessed."[5] This is because the corrupting power of sin, which controlled the will before conversion, was replaced by the truth of the Spirit of grace. The will will be convinced to act when persons understanding is convinced of spiritual truth.

This dramatic change is accomplished by God's spirit of grace. It provokes the mind to "rightly understand" and the will to "freely desire heavenly things." It is this process that puts humans in unity with Christ, according to Reynolds. This is saving faith through (1) humans, concluding that there is no hope within themselves, look to God as able to save them; (2) and they determine to trust no inferior causes of salvation (3 which is followed by a positive decision to trust Jesus Christ. This saving faith radically transforms the inner working of persons' souls.

This is the process Reynolds had in mind as he preached. He could be labeled an "evangelical preacher" because his overriding intention in every sermon was to inculcate this process of "saving faith" in his listeners. He was definitely an evangelist. He was called a moderate Calvinist in that all prescribed behavior for clergy that was not pertaining to essential doctrine could be tolerated and allowed except for independent groups such as Quakers and those groups based on individuals who suddenly decide they are called to preach with no further training or supervision. This moderation

5. Jeremiah, "Edward Reynolds (1599–1676)," 61.

even allowed Reynolds to collaborate with some Anglicans who, themselves, took most of archbishop Laud's recommendations with reservation.

Reynolds was known as one of the best preachers in seventeenth-century Christendom. His sermons were published and read by many. He was only one of a few whose sermons and essays were published while he was still alive.[6]

---

6. Donagan. "Puritan Ministers and Laymen," 81–111. She notes that there were few if any constraints put on ministers in this century, provided what was said was within a sermon.

6

Reynolds at the Westminster
Assembly of Divines

IT WAS DURING THIS Long Parliament that the Assembly of Divines, which Reynolds said he had heard about, occurred. Here again the word "long" is appropriate in that this assembly, which finally began to meet in Westminster during the summer of 1643, did so amidst an extensive period of turmoil among the king, the English Parliament, Ireland, and Scotland.[1] For the next ten years the assembly was one of the major institutions in the United Kingdom. An observer commented that "members of the assembly were often paraded down London streets and feasted at banquets."

Edward Reynolds was among those invited to be a part of the Westminster Assembly but he did not attend the whole first year. His absence was probably due to illness. Throughout his adult life he suffered from the pain of kidney stone obstruction.[2] When he arrived in 1644 he played a moderate, supportive role and entered

---

1. Paul, *Assembly of the Lord* provides a very readable coverage of these events.

2. This was the malady that finally took his life. Interestingly, of the 120 clergy and thirty-six laymen appointed to the assembly, only sixty-nine appeared on the opening day. From 1646 to the end of the assembly, only three times was the vote over thirty-six (half of those appointed).

into every discussion. However, he was not a great debater. The most significant experience he had by far was getting to know and appreciate Scottish Presbyterianism.[3]

This had to have been an eye-opening experience for Reynolds. While Calvinism, understood "generally"—not "specifically"—had characterized much of the Church of England's practice in both James and Charles's reigns, there was no understanding that these efforts would lead to a structure other than the episcopal system inherited by monarch/Parliament agreement after the Pope's replacement by Henry VIII. In fact, at the Hampton Court conference in 1603, James I had declared that the Church of England would *not* be reformed along Puritan or Presbyterian lines. In calling for the Westminster Assembly the House of Commons had stated "this ordinance or anything therein contained shall not give unto the persons aforesaid (the named divine) or any of them any jurisdiction or authority ecclesiastical whatsoever or any power other than that herein expressed . . . The Assembly was to discuss only such matters "as shall be proposed to them by either or both houses of Parliament and no other."[4]

To make matters a bit more confusing, the episcopal system had been abolished in the confusion leading up to the assembly, the divines were called for "the vindicating and clearing of the doctrine of the Church of England of all false calumnies and aspersions." Thus, they were to advise the Parliament on certain ecclesiastical matters. While the divines were not called to recommend a radical new style of church government they were expected to reform the outmoded episcopal one. The best way to conceive of these divines, many of them who would become Presbyterian, is that they could affirm a broad national protestant church which embraced all persons with a simple liturgy, a developing structure and a Calvinist theology.

While Reynolds had very little direct knowledge of the Presbyterian Church of Scotland, he had presumed that it functioned

---

3. Paul, *Assembly of the Lord*, contends that Reynolds could only be labeled "Presbyterian" after, not before, the Westminster Assembly

4. Jeremiah, "Edward Reynolds," 112–13.

in an almost congregational style with no supervision above the local level. He was committed to a "national" church under essentially a supportive monarch. He was not critical of episcopal oversight as can be seen, incidentally, in his later appointment to be the Lord Bishop of Norwich—which he accepted. As deliberations of the assembly developed, Reynolds was encouraged to realize that the Presbyterian Church in Scotland included a form of supervision above the local level. It's term was "synod." There existed in the Scottish Presbyterian Church a number of synods ,each of which were composed of a group of churches that existed under a supervisory director.

His preconception was changed after the assembly discussion of the structure of the New Testament church. The Independents argued that the church was one large congregation, while the Presbyterian position was that in Acts 2, the Jerusalem church consisted of groups of congregations under several Presbyterys or synods. He suggested that when the apostles decided to select deacons, their meeting constituted a Presbytery. This affirmed Reynolds's viewpoint in two ways: its conclusion was rooted in Scripture, and it implied a supervision of separate congregations by a larger church body. While Reynolds insisted no form of church government was divinely determined by God, he did assert a need for a model of accountability in which local bodies were to be understood a parts of a whole.

Of course, Reynolds's preference was that this "larger church body" be ultimately under a person who did function by divine right, i.e., the king. He remained a Royalist throughout his life. Further, he basically affirmed the Episcopal model of church supervision and government. Reynolds and the five other English divines on the Grand Committee voted no in response to the Independents' proposal of a non-hierarchal congregational polity. This negative support for their proposal prompted one group of pilgrims to leave for New England.[5]

---

5. For a complete coverage of the Grand Debate over Presbyterian Church Government, see Paul, *Assembly of the Lord*, 249–60.

As might be expected from Reynolds's preaching notoriety, he was asked to preach to the assembly on October 8, 1645, a fast day, and he chose the topic of self-denial.[6] It reflected a familiar Reynolds's religious theme of the need for the divines to move toward unity and order lest their disharmony become fertile grounds for independence and radicalism. He lamented that ministers had abandoned proper preaching of God's word: i.e., things doctrinal and evangelical. He stressed the importance of "faith, duty, and godliness." He urged unity that didn't focus on small matters. Showing a waning of his support for the king, he urged prayers for Charles—especially any dependence on enemies of the Christian faith.

Reynolds was one of a committee of a few appointed to draft an actual Confession of Faith. This was possibly the most important issue to be determined by the Westminster Assembly. After considerable debate, the composition was narrowed down to seven members, of which Edward Reynolds was one. They were instructed to consult with the four Scots commissioners. Throughout a very complex and taxing process, Reynolds was a member of all three major committees that determined the Confession. Over these discussions, which took two years and three months, Reynolds was the one man who provided a continuing presence.[7]

One issue, church government, became the overriding and divisive concern of the assembly. They finally claimed divine right for the Presbyterian form of government. The rest of the Confession was decided relatively easily. The House of Commons, however, added the requirement that every detail of the of the Confession be given scriptural justification. This took some additional time. Finally, the Confession of Faith was finished and submitted as a report to the assembly on November 26, 1646. This led to assembly debate of the nineteen chapters and a report of the minutes was drafted; the confession of faith was finalized on December 4, 1646. It was then submitted as a committee report to Parliament. The report said that Scripture verses were not attached because

6. See Benedict and Reynolds, *Whole Works of the Right Rev. Edward Reynolds.*

7. Paul, *Assembly of the Lord,* 135–261.

that would cause confusion, and the Confession was a theological document that implied, but should not require, proof texting.[8] The report also stated that it was not possible for the assembly to print the Confession.

This did not stop the House of Commons. They gave the order to print the whole of the Confession of Faith, expecting the assembly to provide the proof texts, which they did on April 27, 1647. The House of Commons then appointed the Westminster Assembly to print six hundred copies. England now had a new Reformed Confession of Faith. Reynolds had a new identity—he was a Presbyterian.

Sections of the Westminster Confession of Faith are as follows:

1.1.1.1. Holy Scriptures

1.1.1.2. Covenant Theology: Christ's Mediation & Free Will

1.1.1.3. Salvation

1.1.1.4. Law, Christian Liberty and Worship

1.1.1.5. Civil Government and Marriage

1.1.1.6. Church

1.1.1.7. Sacraments

1.1.1.8. Church Government and Discipline

1.1.1.9. Eschatology

This Westminster Confession of Faith[9] shaped much of the theology in the American colonies. In 1648 the Congregational Synod of the Massachusetts Bay Colony adopted it, as did the churches in Connecticut. In 1707, American Baptists adopted the Westminster Confession along with its congregational polity and adult believer baptism. The number of children whose primary religious training came from the Westminster Shorter Catechism has surely been in the millions. For over three centuries, the

8. Rogers, *Scriptures in the Westminster*. This volume discusses the issue of Scripture in the Confession of Faith then and now.

9. Williamson, *Westminster Confession of Faith*. Also Williamson, *Westminster Shorter Catechism*.

Westminster Confession and Catechisms were the sole doctrinal standards of British and American Presbyterianism.[10]

The conclusions of the Westminster Assembly are possibly among the most notable contributions that the English Church has made to world—wide Christianity.

10. Cf. Rogers, *Presbyterian Creeds* for this history. He notes that the theology of the Confession was also widely accepted by Congregationalists and many Baptists.

7

The Remonstrance and the
Execution of Charles I

THE WESTMINSTER ASSEMBLY CONSUMED all of Reynolds's time
and energy from 1643–46. It had produced the soon-to-become-
well-known Westminster Confession of faith. In addition it had
produced the Directory for the Public Worship of God and Longer and Shorter Catechisms (the former for public worship and
the shorter for the instruction of children). When he returned
to his Brauston Parish, Reynolds became aware that the tension
between the Long Parliament and King Charles had continued
and, in fact, increased.

In addition to his continued call to Parliament for support
of his Scottish and Irish forays, Charles had further alienated his
subjects by appointing William Laud (1633–45) the chancellor
of Oxford, as Archbishop of Canterbury. Laud was a traditional
Royalist who strongly favored formal worship replete with ritual.
This basically affronted Parliament's Reform/Presbyterian recommendations coming out of the Westminster Assembly. Laud was
accused of being pro-Catholic, which he denied in spite of his
rulings that pleased his Catholic spouse, who would have wished
England had never left Rome. He openly felt Catholicism was the
one true church but reluctantly supported the king, not the Pope,

as head of the church. Nevertheless, Laud infuriated the populace by making communion tables into altars, moving them to the back of the sanctuary, introducing communion rails, and increasing the use of images and candles. He opposed Calvinistic thinking and advocated Arminianism. He was very unpopular with Puritans and advocated Sunday sports. He unilaterally ruled that scores of Church of England priests who did not support his decisions were to be discharged from their parishes.

Parliament took the Laud predicament into its own hands. Without waiting for the final report of the Westminster Assembly, it collaborated with the Scots in 1643 to accept a Solemn League and Covenant. This made the Reform religion uniform across England, Scotland, and Ireland. Further it sought to extirpate "popery" and church government by episcopal bishops. It abolished use of *Book of Common Prayer* and substituted the directory for worship framed by the Westminster Assembly. It established the Presbyterian form of church government. This ended Laudism. He was impeached by the Long Parliament and found guilty. A bill of attainder was passed and, under it, Laud was decapitated in 1645.[1]

This all happened during the final years of the Westminster Assembly without any involvement of Rev. Edward Reynolds. Upon his return to his parish, he did what he did best—i.e., preach. As usual, his was the voice of moderation—this time with a Presbyterian twist. During the 1640s, Reynolds, like almost all Englishmen, was a supporter of the monarchy. By 1645 he was expressing some doubt that Charles was as much the defender of the Protestant faith as he had presumed. Throughout this period Reynolds had evaluated the nation's problems from a spiritual perspective. He expressed the conviction that the nation's problems were the result of the sins of the people. He called for introspection and repentance as the first step for binding up the nation's wounds.

During these years the English Civil War between the monarch and the parliament went on unabated. In 1648 the Parliamentary Army had to fight an army of Royalists that the king

1. Kenneth Scott Latourette details these events in detail in *History of Christianity*, 820.

had recruited. This time, when Charles was captured he was held firmly in hand. The Parliament was done with negotiations. They considered Charles to be "a man of blood" responsible for waging war against his own people. An Act of Remonstrance containing deeds of his guilt was handed down and approved by a "Rump" Parliament of less than 200 members. During the trial, King Charles I refused to recognize the authority of the court and would not enter a plea. He continually tried to speak to the court and attendant crowd but was denied that right by the presiding officer. A verdict of "guilty" was given and signed by only fifty-seven of the remaining 159 commissioners of the high court established by the Rump parliament.. On January 10, 1649 King Charles I was beheaded outside the banqueting house on Whitehall before a crowd of thousands. At that point, Presbyterianism as a political force fell apart.

Reynolds could scarcely believe the reports of the trial in Westminster Hall. He mourned the assassination of Charles. His personal feelings concerning the king's death are revealed in a Latin poem written by Reynolds with John Garden, one of the moderate Anglicans with whom Reynolds had worked for some solution to the impasse between the king and Parliament. It was entitled *The Divine Penitential Meditations and Vows of His Late Majesty, Charles 1, King of England, 1600–1649*. It purported to be the final thoughts of a very pious King Charles I in his solitary imprisonment at Holmby House. Whether Charles was this pious may be doubted, but the poem does reflect his attitude toward his kingship and his understanding of the situation in which he found himself. Even more, it tells us how Reynolds dealt with the warring feelings within himself.

If the question is asked, "Who really wrote this poem?," the answer is both Charles and Reynolds.[2] It is attributed to Charles I and he must have left a kind of outline of what he perhaps would have said at his trial, if given a chance. Charles would have left it to

2. This is generally attributed to Reynolds. On the title page of the 1649 booklet, publisher unknown, is the note that the material was turned into verse by E. R. Gentleman.

be found after his execution. Reynolds would not, by himself, have created a document with this content. It is, however, completely characteristic of Charles. He begins by confessing his sins to God. He admits that his position as king made things worse. But immediately Charles pointed to his own afflictions, comparing them to those of King David. He moves to bargaining with God. If God will show mercy, then Charles would settle true religion, follow law and justice, and suppress schisms in the church and factions in the state.

Charles was never realistic about his position. He always believed that he was God's anointed and that no evil would befall him. He would not settle for some improvement in his situation. He wanted everything to be restored to the way it had been before the Long Parliament and civil wars. He wanted all the ancient rights and glory of his predecessors. One of the most telling of Charles's requests was that God would keep him from ever going against his conscience. It was this intransigence that led, in part, to Charles's own execution.

Charles I's position is given in terse statements in the left-hand column of each of eight pages. Parallel to it is a poem which reflects and softens the content of Charles's outline.

Charles I's final request was that God completely reverse the situation in which he found himself.

> If Lord thou once wilt put again
> The Sword of Justice in my hand
> Impartiality for to remain,
> To punish those who hate Command,
> And a Protector for the good to stand.

Charles added an ending that had an appearance of humility but with a bitter twist: "O may my People ev'ry one, and the Church be happy, if not by me yet without me." Reynolds translated that into a far more gracious wish: "O may my people ev'ry one, And thy pure Church (thy beauteous love). Be happy, let their joy be known, If not by me the sinner let them prosp'rous prove." Charles I, before his execution, unrealistically allowed himself to believe that he could be restored to his kingship. Edward

Reynolds, after Charles's death, indirectly made the statement that things would have been better had there been negotiation and Charles, rather than being killed, might have been given a chance to serve the kingdom in a limited way that was represented by Charles's best intentions For Reynolds, moderation and compromise always presented the best option.

Soon after the death of Charles I, the Parliament sought to confront and overcome the center of his support, the University of Oxford.

8

Reynolds Returns to Oxford as Reformer

AT NO OTHER TIME had Presbyterianism been stronger than during these early days of England—the Commonwealth without a king. The London provincial Assembly functioned as the national headquarters of the Presbyterian Church. They began to create presbyteries and elect Lay Elders. The seeds for calling Edward Reynolds the "Pride of the Presbyterians" were being firmly planted.

Soon after Charles I's death, the Parliament sought to confront and overcome the center of the king's support, the University of Oxford. In fact, the city of Oxford had become the locale of the king's throne and government headquarters. The queen had her entourage in Merton College, and Christ Church was the locale of the king himself. There was a suspicion that a tunnel connected the two. The army stored arms, food, clothing and supplies throughout the colleges. The scholarly role of the university had almost ceased. The number of freshmen as well as graduating students decreased sharply. Soldiers were housed throughout the university and had corrupted student life. After four years of stress, Oxford University, as it had been through the centuries, had almost ceased to exist. The university and the city of Oxford had become the Royalist stronghold of the nation.

The Long Parliament took the reform of Oxford as one of its major endeavors. It was determined to root out the political teachings and monarchist loyalty which were so different from its endeavor to be a commonwealth that housed a renowned university. As Jeremiah observed, "As a result of Archbishop William Laud's influence on it (he had served as the chancellor from April 12, 1629 to June 25, 1641), Oxford was the stronghold of Royalist, Anglo-Catholic ritual, and Arminian theology . . . Joined to Laudianism; it was the political idea of the divine right of the English monarchy."[1]

Compared to the relative ease of the Parliament's military victory over Oxford, the reform of the university was extremely slow. There were twenty-six articles of the surrender treaty signed on June 24, 1646, by Sir Thomas Fairfax, commander of the parliamentary forces. In a separate section regarding the university, the treaty guaranteed that the university would continue to enjoy its ancient form of government. However, the university's rights were subordinated to the "immediate authority and power of the Parliament." Finding a way to accomplish both were the nearly impossible task given to Edward Reynolds.

He was suddenly thrust into the middle of the Parliament's efforts to restore, disassemble, reform, change, and encourage support of the Commonwealth which was trying to rule England without a king. Earlier Reynolds had been called a "Parliament man" because of his agreeing to accept the invitation to participate in the Long Parliament's Assembly of Divines. Now, Reynolds, though still a Royalist at heart, agreed to be one of the seven Church of England ministers, all Oxford graduates, who would go to Oxford and preach in an effort to begin a dialogue. They understood their task was to preach, not argue politics. They thought their chief opposition would be those who espoused Arminianism, so they emphasized the doctrine of justification, regeneration, and grace. They were received with scorn and laughter.

Unexpectedly, they aroused the rivalry of the religious Independents. They were ready to challenge the Presbyterians and assert their views. They took the preaching of the divines as the

---

1. Jeremiah, "Edward Reynolds," 143.

opportunity to state their convictions. The strength and variety of these Independent sects surprised Reynolds. Although he preached moderation and openness to other opinions, he was firmly opposed to many of these opinions. Each of these sects saw no need for seminary education but relied on the Holy Spirit to give them guidance and beliefs. Chief among the Independent opposition was William Erbury. He espoused Socinianism—the position that denied Christ had any church or ministers on earth.

Other groups included "Levelers" or "Diggers." They were begun in 1649 by Gerrard Winstanley, who advocated leveling the social order by implementing an agrarian lifestyle and small rural communities. "Ranters" were pantheists who believed that God was present in every creature. They denied the authority of the church, the Scriptures, and all human leadership. They felt they were in the process of becoming godlike. "Muggletonians" were named after Ludowicke Muggleton, one of two Italian tailors who, in 1751, announced they were the last prophets foretold in the book of Revelation. They believed that God took no notice of what was happening on earth and only intervened to bring the world to an end. "Seekers" believed all churches were corrupt. They held no religious services, but gathered in silence and spoke only if inspired.

Most prominent were the Quakers. They believed that everyone had an inner light that would guide them. One of their leaders, George Fox, attributed the name "Quaker" to a judge who in 1650 "bid them tremble before the Lord." "Fifth Monarchy Men" were unique in their involvement with government. They were critical of government to turn England into a more "godly" nation. They took their name from a prophecy in Daniel 2 that maintained four previous empires had come and gone. The next and last empire would be founded when Jesus Christ returned to earth and ruled with his saints for thousand years.

All of these sects took advantage of the new freedom of religion. Many were millenarians who were sure the end of the world was coming soon.[2] All were seen as threats to the established order

---

2. Jeremiah, *Edward Reynolds*, 211 for this description of the Independents.

of society and government. Most were antinomians who believed that they were free from the law. There were the "Adamites," who believed that, as children of the First Adam, they were free from any restraints. They went around naked until the police placed some restraint on them.

All the Presbyterian ministers preached primarily at St. Mary's Church. They had an open house for questions every week. All their efforts proved unsatisfactory. Parliament had underestimated the opposition of the Royalists and had been totally surprised by the intrusion of the Independents. So, on May 1, nine months after the surrender treaty, Parliament appointed a board of twenty-four visitors for Oxford. Edward Reynolds was among the eight active members. Reynolds's wife began expressing continued dissatisfaction at his involvement in these political affairs.

The visitors were given broad powers. They were to hear and determine all crimes, offenses, and disorders. They were to discover all religious, political, and military opposition to the Commonwealth. They were to report their findings to the London Committee, who would decide how to respond. The chairman was Francis Rous, a well-known parliamentarian and a former member of the Assembly of the Divines.

The Royalists at Oxford responded with a statement that they did not recognize any visitation not authorized by the king (who was non-existent). They also objected to members of the clergy being on the visitation (of which Reynolds was one). They asserted their belief in the doctrine of the Church of England rather than the Westminster Assembly's new Confession of Faith. The London Committee did not reply to this statement, and after twenty months of trying persuasion, resorted to force. Philip, Earl of Pembroke, was appointed chancellor of Oxford, and installed Edward Reynolds as vice chancellor and dean of Christ Church.

On April 1648, Pembroke arrived and expelled Vice Chancellor Fell and his family. In the afternoon he presided over a convocation and installed Reynolds, who promised to observe the statutes, liberties, privileges, and customs rightly established of this university. Reynolds spoke modestly of himself, noting how difficult it was for a man who had sequestered himself from secular employment to be called into government. In reforming the university,[3] Reynolds hoped that "good example and counsel might prevail more . . . than severity and punishment." Reynolds then received a Doctorate of Divinity. He did not accompany Pembroke as he replaced the heads of the Oxford Colleges—a move that enraged the Royalists, who ridiculed him. The only sermon Reynolds published while at Oxford was Animalis Homo in Latin. The Royalist literature pictured Reynolds as a "humble man who did not wish to take a position if it meant the ejection of another person." The visitors then summoned the students from all the colleges and asked them to submit to the visitation. This resulted in 340 students not agreeing, and they were dismissed.

Reynolds did not attend meetings of the London Committee for two months in the spring and early summer. He was probably at home talking with his wife who, once again, was expressing her displeasure at her husband's involvement in the attempts to have the Commonwealth assert its will over Oxford University. There was intense pressure against the university from outside Oxford. The universities (Cambridge as well as Oxford) supported the episcopacy. Others wanted to abolish tithes and livings for ministers. It was natural to want to abolish the universities whose principal function was to train ministers. For many, the Independents especially, all that was needed for a minister was for the Spirit of Christ to fall on him. The knowledge of Latin, Greek, and Hebrew was irrelevant. Oxford and Cambridge were symbols of the elitism of church and society that should be abolished.

Pressure from the London Committee came from those who wanted more aggressive action. Under Reynolds's leadership, a more lenient policy was adopted toward those Royalists who remained as head of colleges and students. They could keep their places, but not their votes or positions as teachers. This meant decreasing the intrusion of the visitors into university affairs. On January 22, 1649, the fellows of Exeter College requested the

3. This could be one reason why the only sermon Reynolds published during his time at Oxford was in Latin, "Animalis Homo" (1649).

right to elect a new rector, since their rector had died. The visitors deemed this request "very just and reasonable." This was the first time the visitors did not intervene in the election of a new head. Under Reynolds, ordinary studies were resumed as soon as possible. Latin and Greek were the only languages that were to be spoken by teacher or student. Reynolds encouraged Simon Lord, a fellow Magdalen, to publish his sermon in Latin. Even Royalists generally agree that Reynolds had done much to restore Oxford to university standards.

The Presbyterians had three principal concerns for university learning: Reform worship, strict morality, and godly learning. Reynolds sought to accomplish these ends with mixed results. In April 1648, the Book of Common Prayer was prohibited. Catechizing from the Westminster Confession of Faith was often done. Prayers were offered in the rooms of many tutors at night. The strictness of Presbyterian morals was evidenced in expulsion and swearing. Public drunkenness was severely punished. Students were not to eat in public places on fast days. Bed makers were required to be "ancient women" of good report. All of this contributed to a context in which the desired "godly learning" could take place.

In his dedication to "Animalis Homo," the only sermon Reynolds had published while at Oxford, he acknowledged his initial resistance to taking on the administrative work at Oxford, he predicted he would retreat in retirement in the country and take refuge for some days among books and be set free from this thing. Instead. Reynolds did a work in reforming Oxford in a moderate manner with leniency toward his Royalist opposition. He modeled in his action what he preached in his sermons.

9

Reynolds and the Commonwealth

POLITICS AGAIN INTERVENED AND ultimately forced Reynolds to leave Oxford. In late 1649, following the death of the king, Parliament decided that some new vow of loyalty was needed. It was decided that on October 11 all members of the Rump Parliament should take an "engagement" in the following words:

"I do declare and promise, that I will be true and faithful to the Commonwealth of England, as the same is now established, without a King or House of Lords."

The taking of the engagement went so smoothly with the Rump Parliament that it was decided to require it of all public officials, members of professional classes, and clergy applying for benefices. By the following January, the decision was made to require it of everyone in the country.

Presbyterians, especially the clergy, were the chief opponents to the engagement. For them, it contradicted their subscription to the solemn league and covenant in which they promised to protect the king's person and that of his heirs. The engagement implied that they approved the execution of the king. Without that implication, they would probably have been willing to support the current government.

Francis Rous, chairman of the London Committee and a Presbyterian "one that loves all Presbyterian lovers of truth and peace," wrote a pamphlet entitled "The Lawfulness of Obeying the Present Government" in which he noted that some obligations might end. He was referring to the death of the king, which he felt was no longer binding. Reynolds wrote "Humble Proposals of Sunday and Pious Divines" on behalf of the Presbyterian ministers. It served as a response to Rous. Reynolds began by affirming that as ministers of the gospel of Jesus, they had all faithfully served the Parliament, pursued liberty and reformation, and suffered from the common enemy. Further, they still adhered to their first principles, maintained the peace of the nation and were obedient to the laws thereof. Yet, he felt taking the engagement would do great harm for those who had taken the solemn league and covenant. It would make it appear that the ministers were unstable. And it would ruin ministers and their families. Reynolds did not dispute the legality of the Commonwealth government and called for a public debate so that ministers could clear their consciences.

The debate was held on February 15 and March 1, 1650. Participants were non-subscribing Presbyterian ministers and Independent supporters of the engagement. It was non-conclusive, in part because there were no Independent ministers that dealt theologically with the scruples of the Presbyterians.

However, Reynolds, in his role as vice-chancellor of Oxford, indicated he was willing to take the engagement. Yet a meeting of the university convocation decided that a petition should be drawn up for the sake of those who had scruples against the engagement. They petitioned Parliament purely on the basis of conscientious principles. They asked if it would be sufficient to declare and promise that they would live peaceably in their places and callings under the present government. Unfortunately, this petition was rejected by the London Committee and never reached the Parliament.

Given that situation, Reynolds and his friends were faced with the choice of "sin," accepting the engagement, or "affliction," losing their places at Oxford. Reynolds, along with other Presbyterian visitors, refused to sign the engagement. Christopher Rogers was put in Reynolds's position as vice chancellor of Oxford. Reynolds hoped to retain his position as dean of Christ Church, but was ejected from it, as well, in March 1651. Interestingly, Reynolds's wife, in spite of some reluctance she experienced to being there in the first place, was reluctant to leave the university quarters in which she had been living and had to be forcibly removed—as had the wife of the previous vice chancellor who he had replaced. Truth is often stranger than fiction!

In his dedication to "Animalis Homo," Reynolds acknowledged his initial resistance to taking on the administrative work at the university. He predicted he would retreat in retirement to the country and take refuge among books when the turmoil had ceased. Then he would be set free from this task. Instead, Reynolds had done a work in reforming Oxford in a moderate manner with leniency toward the Royalist opposition. He modeled in his action what he preached in his sermons.

At no time during the seventeenth century was Presbyterianism in higher regard. Nor was there a moment in which Edward Reynolds was more deserving of being labeled "Pride of the Presbyterians."

Reynolds did, indeed, retire to the rural life of Braunston, his long-time parish. But points of interest continued to show up in Reynolds's life. A second edition of his *Treatise of the Passions and Faculties of the Soule of Man* was published in 1651. It had become a text in the Oxford curriculum.. He, also, was able to give more time to family matters. A great joy for him was the marriage of his youngest daughter, Elizabeth, to John Conant in August, 1651.

In some ways Conant's life paralleled Reynolds's. They both had come from lower-middle-class backgrounds. Conant, too, served All Saints in Northampton and, at times, was head of Exeter College and vice chancellor of Oxford. Further, as political winds shifted and demands for conformity were made and refused, Conant, like Reynolds, was ejected from the positions he had assumed. Some years later, Conant was ordained priest by Reynolds, who had become Bishop of Norwich by that time.

After several years in semi-retirement, Reynolds returned to the national spotlight by accepting the call to one of the six most prominent and influential parishes in the country—St. Laurence Jewry in London. As Jeremiah reported, "From the platform this church provided, Reynolds's message of moderation and his call for peace and stability in political and religious affairs drew great support, and catapulted him back into a position of national leadership in the late 1650's." He became a preacher in great demand. For example, in addition to his Sunday sermon and Thursday lecture, he preached to the political and business leadership of the nation on many occasions This included eight times to the London corporation, three times to Parliament and once to the East India Company. His message of peace, unity, and moderation was well received.

In his sermon entitled "Joy in the Lord," Reynolds stated, "We live in changeable and unsettled times, we see distempers, we hear of distresses abroad . . . I say rejoice; I speak it by commission of the mouth of Christ, requiring it; I speak it by the experience of mine own heart, enjoying it in the midst of all my sufferings." He used his sickness as an illustration in this sermon. He noted, "bring the richest pearl to a man under some fit of gout or stone, he cries, groans, sweats . . . It would be little good to such a man, to tell him that his kidneys or his bladder were full of pearls or diamonds, because they would not be his treasure, but his torment."[1]

Further, Reynolds treats the learned ministry as the sole bearers of the message of Salvation. He described a person's attitude toward a minister as equivalent to that person's attitude toward Christ. He was still perceived as a moderate in a culture where Roman Catholicism on the one side and uneducated sectarians on the other seemed to deny the most basic beliefs of the Protestant Christian faith. He concluded by claiming "that the wounds of Christ are better than with the kisses of the world; it is much better being with a frowning father, than a flattering foe; the worst estate of a saint is better than the best of a sinner."[2]

Reynolds believed that government had an important role to play in religious affairs. It should establish and protect the Christian religion. Magistrates should exercise coercive power in

1. Jeremiah, *Edward Reynolds*, 192.
2. Jeremiah, *Edward Reynolds*, 193.

controlling the religious behavior among the populace. This was termed the erastian point of view. Jeremiah noted that Reynolds preached there should be five duties of magistrates: "(1) to protect and promote the saving truths agreed to by the Reformed churches, (2) to comfort and encourage godly, sober and peaceable ministers, (3) to preserve and vindicate schools of learning for ministers, (4) to discourage and prevent dangerous and pernicious doctrines, and (5) to provide an able, resident ministry for all the 'dark and ignorant places' of the land." He told the Parliament that peace depended on obliging people to "attend upon the ministry and dispensation of the Gospel" in some Christian assembly.[3] Parliament subsequently passed the Sabbath Observance Act which required all English persons to attend church every week. He said he would implore God to give them strength to enforce this. Reynolds never ceased to support a national church to support these points of view.

Reynolds was well received by the businessmen at St. Laurence Jewry as well as those in the larger London community. He was called to speak to the Lord Mayor and London business leaders on how to be wise merchants in the city of God as well as in the world. His sermon was called "True Gain." His text was Matthew 16:26: "For what is a man profited, if he shall gain the whole world, and lose his own soul? Or what shall a man give in exchange for his soul?" He declared: "I shall reduce all unto this one proposition: As Christ allows his servants to be moved by consideration of gain in his service, so he does withal assure us, that this gain does not stand in winning the world, but in saving of the soul; . . . therefore a wise Christian should have his trade heavenward for the enriching of his soul, rather than downward for the possession of the world."[4]

Reynolds then developed a lengthy analogy to show that a wise Christian must behave shrewdly as a wise merchant. "The wisest merchants must live by faith, and deal much in credit, waiting long for a good return out of remote countries . . . Such

3. Jeremiah, *Edward Reynolds*, 410, 193.
4. Jeremiah, *Edward Reynolds*, 194.

is the life of a true Christian, he does not estimate his wealth by the things in his own possession, but lives by faith, reckons upon a great stock going in another country, is richer in obligations and promise, then he is in present graces. There is a mutual trust between God and him . . . Finally, to conclude all, the life of a merchant in order to gain stands in these four things: In wisdom, and forecast to contrive; in labor, to transact business; in patience to wait; and in thriftiness to preserve what his labors gain: So our Christian labors."[5]

In the meantime, the structural life of the Commonwealth had taken a firmer shape. Oliver Cromwell had been the commander of the Parliamentary armies at the time of the execution of King Charles I. A political vacuum occurred. Cromwell gradually found himself in line to assume the leadership of the government. Parliament recognized the situation and suggested he become king, but he refused and took instead the title of Lord Protector. The government took the name of the Commonwealth and became a kind of republic.

Cromwell was a relative unknown to Reynolds, but what he learned about him started out to be good. Although a soldier, Cromwell was a deeply religious man who believed in a national church and religious tolerance. He tended to affirm Independents and was open to all Protestants except Quakers. He did not support the episcopacy and outlawed the Book of Common Prayer. His only desire was that the word was to be preached and ministers were to be supported by tithes and offerings. Even Catholics could meet if they did so quietly. Cromwell gave England the nearest thing to religious tolerance it had previously known.

Reynolds never changed his intolerance of Catholics and Quakers. Reynolds was greatly disturbed by the idea of sending troops to put down the Irish rebellion, however. The rebellion had started in Ulster, but spread quickly through the whole kingdom. Catholics were in charge everywhere. Cromwell ruthlessly attacked Ireland, killing both Protestants and Catholics alike. There were reports of Presbyterian babies impaled, and Cromwell's troops

5. Jeremiah, *Edward Reynolds*, 195.

committed the worst atrocities in English history. Cromwell testified that he intended a slaughter so terrible that no military force would dare to stand in his way.

When the news reached London, Reynolds felt sickened by the excesses he had failed to expect of Cromwell. The Council of State recalled Cromwell in April 1650. He returned to England a hero. But Cromwell was not done with war. Charles II, the late king's son, appeared in Scotland to take the throne offered him by the Royalist Scots. He was a most unlikely Puritan or Presbyterian and, at twenty years of age, had already begun to father children by a long list of mistresses. Although outnumbered, Cromwell took the fight to the Scots. He lured the Scots deep into English territory when they believed people would rally to the Royalist cause. The Commonwealth troops massacred the Royalist-Scottish forces. Disguised, Charles II escaped back to exile in Paris. Reynolds, like many other Englishmen, admired Charles II's creativity.

This was a tumultuous time. Cromwell replaced the Rump Parliament with a nominated assembly handpicked by his own army council. It came to be known as Cromwell's Barebones Parliament after a take off a member's name: "Barbon." Many in the assembly were excitable Independents looking for the last days before Christ's return. Cromwell played into their preoccupations by stating they were "on the edge of promises and prophecies." Some assembly members talked of replacing all human laws by the Ten Commandments and abolishing all tithes in support of clergy.

Cromwell grew tired of the rhetoric and inaction of the Barebones Parliament. He dismissed the Barebones Parliament and four days later had himself sworn in anew as "Lord Protector" who ruled by a single person (himself) and Parliament. Beginning in 1654, a Protectorate Parliament was to be elected every three years and sit for five months of each year. Their action was to be heavily influenced by the wishes of the Lord Protector—Oliver Cromwell himself.

The apparent stability of the Protectorate did not last long. In response to perceived Royalist plots, in the spring of 1655, Cromwell imposed direct military rule on the counties. These military leaders became morality police. They were strict in enforcing laws of Sabbath observance, drunkenness, swearing, and betting. They tried to suppress cock fights, horse races, brothels, and illegal ale houses, Their attempts failed. Cromwell's constituency, the county gentry, were alienated. In the parliamentary elections, Cromwell's supporters were defeated.

Reynolds, in turn, had preached to large and influential bodies of citizens in 1657 and 1658 without any mention of the political situation, except in the most general way. These were Presbyterian sermons quite unlike those being preached by the Independent sects. Reynolds asked for personal reformation and for using one's influence for the betterment of society. He did not ask for change in the structure of society or in the hierarchy of persons with the king at the top. Five months later an event occurred that radically changed the political context, and that would dramatically refocus the audiences to whom Reynolds would speak, and the message that he would declare.

Oliver Cromwell died on September 3, 1658. A tornado-like storm hit England that day, tearing up trees and toppling church steeples. Some claimed it was the devil come to take Cromwell's soul, which he had sold for supreme power.

The embalming was botched, but an effigy had been made of the body. It was exposed for a lying-in state at Somerset House, robed in purple, with a crown on his head and an orb and scepter in his hands. The kingship he refused in life was imposed on him in death.

The November 23 state funeral was a fiasco. The arguments over protocol so delayed the seven-hour procession through London by the time it arrived at Westminster Abbey, it was nearly pitch dark, and there was an inadequate supply of candles. So the funeral ended with no sermons, prayers, or funeral orations. After two sharp blasts of a trumpet, the effigy was bundled into a waiting tomb. Effectively, the era of the Protectorate was over.

10

Reynolds as Reconciler in the Midst of Chaos

EDWARD REYNOLDS DID NOT grieve the death of Oliver Cromwell, the Lord Protector, as he had that of Charles I, the King. Cromwell had named his eldest surviving son, Richard, as his successor. Whereas Reynolds and other Presbyterian leaders had not sought favor from Oliver Cromwell, at his death they quickly turned to his son Richard.

On October 11, 1658, Edward Reynolds, acting with the support of other Presbyterian ministers, made an oral address to the new Lord Protector. Knowing that Richard was said to have Presbyterian sympathies, they hoped that the government might be willing to revise the statutes on religion in the direction of a national (Presbyterian) establishment.

Ominously, the day after Reynolds's address to the new Lord Protector, the Independents began a twelve-day meeting called the Savoy Assembly. Mostly lay delegates from over one hundred independent congregations met at the Savoy to clarify and strengthen the Independent position. Six divines were on a committee charged with drawing a Confession of Faith. The Savoy Declaration was a modification of the Westminster Confession of Faith completed at the 1646. There was a new chapter entitled "Of the Gospel, and the

Extent of the Grace Thereof." The declaration limited the ability of the civil magistrates to abridge the liberty of those who differed from others through the exercise of good conscience. Most importantly, the declaration replaced chapters 30 and 31 of the Westminster Confession of Faith with a lengthy and elaborate platform of the Congregational church order, entitled, "The Institution of Churches, and the Order Appointed in Them by Jesus Christ."

While these differences from Presbyterian theology might seem slight, the effect was to draw a line between Presbyterians and Independents. Any discussions of religious unity between them were suddenly terminated in 1659. It also thrust John Owen into the spotlight as the Independent's leader just as Edward Reynolds was the leader of the Presbyterians. Reynolds continued to look for a way to work with Richard Cromwell. In direct opposition, John Owen and other Independents joined the army council in opposing him. Reynolds continued to encourage everyone to agree on the main fundamentals of the faith and to live in mutual love, toleration, and forbearance of one another in differences which were not subversive unto faith and godliness while Owen contended that God had broken any desire for the government to engage in any imposition of discipline on worship in the church. Owen's emphatic articulation of the Independents' difference from the Presbyterians drove the Presbyterians, such as Reynolds, toward moderate Anglicans.

The difference between Reynolds and Owen was rooted, in part, in their early upbringing and education. Like Reynolds, John Owen's fees to grammar school and later to Queen's College, Oxford were paid by an uncle. Although Edward Reynolds was influenced by the general Calvinistic atmosphere of Merton rather than any single professor, Owen was decisively impacted by his tutor at Queens, Thomas Barlow, a distinguished Aristotelian scholar. This experience led Owen to recall his Puritan upbringing, where he remembered his father as a "nonconformist all his days"—one who would not submit to the government's regulation of religion. Owen reacted negatively to many of Laud's religious impositions and left Oxford in 1637. He was searching for the assurance that came from Scholastic Calvinism that only individual predestination eventually brought.

Owen held three pastoral charges, all during the period of the civil war. Additionally, he preached at St. Margaret's Westminster to the House of Commons on a fast day, April 29, 1642. His published sermon was entitled "A Vision of Unchangeable Free Mercy in Sending the Means of Grace to Undeserving Sinners." His major theme was that whatever happens on earth is controlled by the will and counsel of God. Between 1644 and 1646 Owen called himself a Presbyterian and tried to find a mediating position between "the Congregational Way" and the "Presbyterian Way." A decade later, Owen had become a convinced Congregationalist and a supporter of the Synod of Dort.

Owen was one of two ministers appointed to preach on the fast day, January 30, 1649, the day of Charles I's execution. The fast was delayed by one day. On the day after the king's execution, Owen preached to the Parliament a sermon entitled "Righteous Zeal Encouraged by Divine Protection" on Jeremiah 15:19-20. He concluded that what *had* happened and what *was* happening was of the Lord. He quoted Psalm 118:23: "This is the Lord's doing and it is marvelous in our eyes." Reynolds was appalled.

Unfortunately for Owen, his republican political views brought him into conflict with Oliver Cromwell. Owen strongly opposed the idea of Cromwell becoming king. He even wrote a petition against monarchy, which the senior army officers presented to Cromwell. From that point until Cromwell's death, Cromwell and Owen had little contact.

Understandings of government and peoples' attitudes toward it changed several times during the Interregnum—that time in England where the Parliament and Protectorate ruled. Various terms were used to describe what the government was after the death of Charles I. At first, England was a republic, in which the authority for government rested entirely with the people and their elected representatives. The Rump Parliament fit this view. As time passed, leaders of the Rump and others preferred to define the government as a Commonwealth, a government dedicated to the welfare of the whole community. Those who wanted a more visible central authority were glad when Cromwell was named Lord Protector and the government was named a Protectorate.

As time passed, attitudes changed, and some, like John Owen, who had been so close to Cromwell, now feared his authority, and longed for a republic in which authority rested directly in the people. In religion, congregationalism, where all authority resided in the local congregation, was advocated. This was Owen's preference and was favored in New England. A more extreme form of this reaction to human government authority was exemplified in the Fifth Monarchy, which held out for a government directly ruled by a returned Jesus Christ. All of these shifting currents of opinion provided a chaos that led many to desire the return of the monarchy.

During this time when Owen was focused on working with the army and supporting Oliver Cromwell, Edward Reynolds and the Presbyterians were in a waiting posture. They did not vocally oppose the Protectorate, nor did they enthusiastically support it. When the king was executed, the Presbyterians essentially dissolved as a working political body. They became many different groups with no unifying agenda.

Reynolds and others, who increasingly depended on some sort of cooperation with the Anglicans, could not agree among themselves as to the conditions for the restoration of the king and Anglicanism. It was finally their reaction against the army and their memory of the early days of the Republic that united these moderate Presbyterian and moderate Anglicans together in support of the restoration of Charles II. These events are a story all their own.

During the short time Richard Cromwell was Lord Protector, General Monck, commander of the Scottish army, was fearful of what the English army might do. He advised Richard Cromwell to balance the radicals by making alliance with some of the Presbyterian divines such as Reynolds and his colleagues. This he did by inviting them to preach at the opening session of the Protectorate Parliament. There were forty Royalist members of Parliament who, as yet, did not trust the Presbyterians to support the return of a king. The army forced Richard Cromwell to dissolve the parliament on April 22, 1659. Richard was forced to abdicate in addition. The army attempted to restore order by recalling the Rump Parliament. This action caused the Presbyterians to begin to cooperate, first with each other, and then with the Royalists against the army council and the Rump Parliament.

William Prynne, former leader of the House of Commons in the days of Parliament's dominance, declared, "The only permanent solution was to restore the 'ancient, hereditary, just legal Kingship with all their necessary invaded Prerogatives, Lands, Revenues, Rights, Jurisdictions' and to preserve them inviolably. Such a government would be a mixture of the three known forms of polity, absolute monarchy, aristocracy, and democracy, with the inconveniences of none."

11

Reynolds and the Restoration
of the Monarch

When Reynolds turned again to comment on the condition of the country, his assessment was more negative and full of cautionary advice. He preached a sermon at St. Paul's before the Lord Mayor, Alderman, and Company of London on November 5, 1659. The text was Zechariah 3:1–2: "And the Lord said to Satan, 'The Lord rebuke thee, O Satan, even the Lord that hath chosen Jerusalem, rebuke thee. Is not this a Brand plucked out of the fire?" Reynolds had London in mind when he spoke of Jerusalem. He said, "We live in failing times . . . We trusted too much in Parliaments, and they have been broken, our Trades broken, our Estates broken, our Government broken, our hopes broken. A sad thing that a people will be quite fatherless before they will think of going to God."

Reynolds continued: "And are not Religion and Laws the best part of a structure, the Foundation? Are not Princes, Peers, Nobles, Fathers of their Country, choice stones in a building? They [the sects] would have turned things upside down, . . . down with Laws, up with confusion: down with Jerusalem, up with Babylon; down with Peers, and Gentry, and Ministry, the flower of a Nations . . .

Tell me whether any but Heads and Hearts filled with the Devil could ever have invented or executed so Bloody a Design?"[1]

One month later, December 2, 1659, in the same place and to the same body, Reynolds preached a warning even more dire. This time his text was Hosea 9:12: "Yea, woe also to them when I depart from them." Reynolds asked a question: "Will changes in government mend us? Will a democracy, or aristocracy. Or any other form of polity mend us, of God be going away from us?" Finally, he proposed a solution: "Resolve every man with Joshua, 'As for me and my house, we will serve the Lord.' [Josh 24:14] The way to keep God in a nation, is for every man to keep God in his own heart, and in his own family first."[2]

The London clergy, led by Reynolds, sent forth a tract on January 23, 1660 warning of the dangerous state of religion. It was entitled: "A Reasonable Exhortation of Sunday Ministers in London to the People of Their Congregations." Just as they had feared that Rome had hidden behind the skirts of Anglicanism in the 1640s, now they believed that Rome was behind the sectaries, especially the Quakers. The statement acknowledged that popery and Quakerism seemed to be at the opposite extremes from each other. However, the argument was that "we cannot but observe a ready coincidence with Papists in their opinions."[3]

While this warning tract was being prepared and distributed, General Monck and his Scottish army arrived in London. Monck's first act was to restore the Long Parliament. Reynolds preached a sermon on a day of solemn thanksgiving unto God for restoring the Parliament and Common Council, and for preserving the city. It was entitled "The Wall and Glory of Jerusalem, in St. Paul's Church, London before the Right Honorable The Lord Mayor, Lord General, Alderman, Common Council, and Companies of the Honorable City of London." He began, "When we consider the

1. Jeremiah, *Edward Reynolds*, 205.

2. Jeremiah, *Edward Reynolds*, 206.

3. A detailed discussion of Presbyterians in this period is found in Abernathy, "English Puritans and the Stuart Restoratio." He is clear on the central role that Reynolds played in Moving Presbyterians forward.

maturity of our mighty Sin, have great reason to fear his Wrath, and when we observe the progress of his Wonderful works, we have some comfortable Encouragement to hope for the renewal of his Mercy. And that so much the rather, because he hath stirred up in your hearts in this great City to return unto him the glory due unto his name for his goodness to these Nations, in restoring the Parliament and unto your selves, in restoring your Council, and healing the Wound inflicted on the Honor of this Renowned City." His text was Zachariah 2:5: "For I, saith the Lord, will be unto her a Wall of Fire round about, and will be the Glory in the midst of her." He ended by proclaiming, "Above all things, hold fast God and his presence. A City is never without Wall or Gates, without glory and splendor, till they are without God."

Reynolds made his final appeal by linking the troubles past with hope for the future in the return of the members of the Long Parliament. His closing rhetorical flourish lifted up the leaders of London as those would assure God's mercies into the future. He proclaimed, "for I am persuaded it is the sober Truth, that no city in the Christian World hath a more glorious presence of God by this Light of his Word, and the purity of his Worship and the Ordinances than London has had . . . So make it your business in an answerable proportion to bring Glory to God . . . give Glory to him and he will be Glory to you."[4] This must have been emotionally stirring to his hearers.

On the same day, the House of Commons appointed a Committee on Religion. Contrary to past practice, no clergymen were appointed. Perhaps to remedy this situation, the London Presbyterian Clergy, on March 1, presented their recommendations to the House of Commons. As expected, they recommended suppression of popery, strict Sabbath observances, a committee to approve ministers, a bill to protect ministers in their benefices, adoption of the Westminster Confession of Faith, and the convening of a national assembly of divines. None of these suggestions offered any conciliation with either Anglicans or the Independents.

---

4. Jeremiah, *Edward Reynolds*, 215–17.

On March 5, Edward Harley, the chair of the Committee for Religion, requested Reynolds and five others to consult with the Committee. A bill to settle ministers in their livings was passed on March 16. The Westminster Confession was adopted with Presbyterian government. Presbyterian clergy were still in place, but with ill will from both the Anglicans and the Independents who were left out of the settlement.

The general assumption was that the monarch would be restored, but no conditions were prescribed that would in any way set boundaries on his power. All engagements except the Solemn League and Covenant were repealed. Given all this, it was understandable that Presbyterians were becoming more open to some compromise with episcopacy. Laudians were growing stronger in their determination to make no concessions. Some among both the Presbyterians and the Anglicans were committed to reconciliation. Prominent among them were Edward Reynolds and John Gauden. Both had been ordained before the Civil War.

The reconstituted Long Parliament dissolved itself. There was only a month to elect members of the new so-called Convention Parliament. By English law, only the sovereign could call a Parliament. When there was no sovereign, then a Convention Parliament was elected to express the will of the people. The business of a Convention Parliament was to make necessary preparation for the restoration of the monarch. First came the decision to call a monarch, and whom to call, and then to deal with necessary matters such as funding that enable the new regime to operate.

The Presbyterians failed to mount a vigorous campaign for persons favorable to them to be elected. The alienation of Presbyterians from Independents and the total rejection of Roman Catholics became an act of political suicide for the Presbyterians. There were no cases of Presbyterian-Independent candidates. In every case where the Presbyterians clashed with an openly Royalist candidate, the Presbyterians lost. Presbyterians seemed oblivious to the changed temperament of the electorate. Royalists were elected in the majority. Public opinion favored the quick return of

Charles II, with or without terms. But few expected a full Laudian form of episcopacy to come with it.

However, the Presbyterians were encouraged when Charles II issued the Declaration of Breda from his place of exile in the United Netherlands. This declaration was prepared by Charles and his advisors. It begins "that we can never give over the hope, in good time, to obtain the possession of that right which God and nature hath made our due, so we make it our daily suit to the Divine Providence that He will . . . put us into a quiet and peaceable possession of that right . . . nor do we desire more to enjoy what is ours, than that all our subjects may enjoy what by law is theirs, be a full and entire administration of justice throughout the land, and be extending our mercy where it is wanted and deserved."[5]

Charles then promised "a free and general pardon" to those who applied within forty days, excepting only such persons as shall hereafter be excepted by Parliament."[6] Charles understood from the outset that anyone who had a part in the execution of his father was excepted from the pardon. He also stated that "we do declare a liberty to tender consciences, and that no man shall be disqualified or called in question for differences of opinion in matters of religion, which do not disturb the peace of the kingdom."[7]

Parliament later decided that allowing any non-Anglican to hold public office would be a threat to the peace of the kingdom. Between 1660 and 1665, the Parliament passed four statutes that became known as the Clarendon Code. They severely restricted the rights of Roman Catholics and nonconformists, such as Puritans. Reynolds personally found favor with the new Council of State, which chose him to preach at the opening of the Convention Parliament.

On that day, April 25, 1660, Reynolds preached on "The Author and Subject of Healing." He stated: "I thought it my duty, as a Minister of the Gospel of Peace, and a Servant of our Great Lord, whose work it was to heal and recover, Luke 4:18, humbly to set

---

5. Jeremiah, *Edward Reynolds*, 228.

6. Jeremiah, *Edward Reynolds*, 229.

7. Jeremiah, *Edward Reynolds*, 267.

before you, the Right Honorable House of Peers, the means and method of God's healing a sick nation."[8] He implored the Convention to show "all possible tenderness and indulgence toward the infirmities, especially the consciences of men of humble and sober, of quiet and peaceable Spirits."[9] At the same time Reynolds emphasized his usual theme, urging the establishment of the "True Reformed Religion and Orthodox, learned and painful Ministry, pure Worship, and the Power of Godliness, suppressing and putting to shame all profane practices."[10]

On May 8, Parliament declared that Charles II was the lawful monarch, and had been since the death of his Father, Charles I, on January 10, 1649. All England was aware that Charles II would soon return as the reigning king of England. Most were overjoyed.

8. Jeremiah, *Edward Reynolds*, 232.
9. Jeremiah, *Edward Reynolds*, 233.
10. Jeremiah, *Edward Reynolds*, 234.

12

Reynolds and the New King

WITH THE CHOICE OF the new English Monarch in place, Reynolds was propelled into action. He realized that the only hope of a religious settlement that included Presbyterianism was to take their concerns directly to the king. During a meeting of some eighty Presbyterian ministers, Reynolds urged that a delegation be sent immediately to dialogue with the king. On May 11, Edward Reynolds and several others departed London and sailed to Holland. No record exists of exactly what the Presbyterians hoped to accomplish. Sir Thomas Wharton wrote a long letter on their behalf in which he described Reynolds as a "very learned, pious, moderate man."

Charles and his advisors responded by receiving the Presbyterians very cordially. The king spoke very respectfully to them and reminded them of the promises he had made in the Declaration of Breda. Reynolds and the others in the delegation returned from Holland with the conviction that Charles would insure their comprehension within the national church. This meant two religious systems within the Church of England—Presbyterianism and Episcopacy.

Toleration of others outside the Established Church was never discussed with the king. Independents, however, rested their hopes in the king's offer of a general toleration. Some irreconcilable Presbyterians who wanted no compromise with episcopacy tried to make common cause with the Independents. Independents turned a cold shoulder to them, not wanting to compromise their own position. The divide was clear from the middle of May. Presbyterians wanted comprehension within the national church. Independents wanted toleration outside a national church.

This was the situation when Charles II and his advisors decided it was time for him to take the throne. A letter by Charles II, sent from Breda, can be seen as evidence that Charles's conversations with Reynolds and the Presbyterian delegation were effective in convincing Charles II of the support of the Presbyterians.

Back in England, things were not perfectly settled. The leading politicians were eager for the stability that a restored monarchy would bring. The Anglicans, especially the Bishops, were ecstatic at the possibility of the restoration of their power. Neither the Independents nor the Presbyterians could decide on the conditions they might prefer. Nevertheless, on May 29, 1660, Charles II's birthday, he entered London accompanied by a dazzling array of twenty thousand cavalry, foot soldiers, and the entirety of the king's court.

Some wept as the stern discipline of the Protectorate society was quickly replaced by debauchery and drunkenness, led by the king himself. Charles was completely immoral. He had many mistresses and a score of illegitimate offspring. How did Edward Reynolds reconcile his own beliefs with King Charles II's behavior? Reynolds gave a major sermon specifically condemning fornication. Yet Charles's fornications were extravagant, open, and seemed endless. Reynolds did not publicly rebuke the king for this sin.

Charles II believed strongly in the divine right of kings. The simplicity of the choice to restore the king was replaced by an enormous complexity in a struggle between the king and the power of a Royalist parliament. Reynolds and the Presbyterians were plunged into a political maelstrom which they could neither understand fully, nor influence effectively.

For the rest of 1660, three parties conducted an intricate dance. The king attempted to craft a compromise which would include Presbyterians in the national church and establish his own prerogative over religion. The restored Anglican bishops were determined to accept nothing less than a return to Laud's high-church religious settlement. The Convention Parliament moved inexorably toward a religious settlement they developed and dictated. Charles, however, had taken matters into his own hands and away from Parliament. He had his own plan, and it evidently included the Presbyterians. This was displayed on June 5 when Charles appointed Reynolds and ten others to be royal chaplains. The king attempted to force the Anglicans to negotiate with the moderate Presbyterians. He made several efforts through called meetings between the two, to little effect. He instructed each side to draw up a set of proposals on church government that he, personally, would read and make decisions among them.

Reynolds was so impressed with this move on the king's part that he preached a sermon at St. Margaret's using Zachariah 4:6's well-known verse "Not by might, not by power, but by my Spirit, saith the Lord of Hosts." In his sermon, Reynolds rehearsed the horrors of the civil war and then declared, "And now comes the Spirit of the Lord to stop this career of domination." He then asked the Parliament "to bless the Lord" for the many virtuous actions that Charles had already taken. According to Reynolds, God had impressed upon the king's heart to do all the things promised in the Declaration of Breda and more. The Presbyterians were very confident that things were going their way.[1]

However, when Reynolds presented a dedicatory preface to this sermon, he noted that he and the other Presbyterians had received the King's command to draw up some materials that would heal "the breaches of the church of God amongst us." This they had done on July 10 when they proposed a form of Usher's reduced episcopacy (bishops as conveners of presbyters who were to advise them). They also requested that kneeling at the Lord's Supper and the observance of holy days be made optional. In addition, they

1. Jeremiah, *Edward Reynolds*, 245.

asked that several practices be abolished: the use of the surplice, the cross in baptism, and bowing at the name of Jesus. These were at the heart of the Presbyterian opposition to the innovations of Archbishop Laud in the 1630s. The bishops answered in writing, stating that all the ceremonies were lawful, there were no abuses in the present system, and giving in to the requests would provoke great dissatisfaction in many people. Reynolds was greatly displeased. In his anger, he stated, "it is wrong if we be zealous for mint and cumin and phylacteries and precepts of men, and have not a proportionable fervor of zeal for the Magnalia Dei: Certainly God will yet reckon with us, and call us to account for all the blood which hath been shed, for all the Treasure which hath been exhausted, for all the Judgments and mercies, for all the providences and wonders which have been expended upon us." In a special thought directed toward the king, Reynolds added, "The Lord be with you while you be with him, and if you seek him, he will be fond of you, but if you forsake him, he will forsake you. The Lord shine upon all your Counsels. Your most humble and devoted in all duty and obedience, Edward Reynolds."[2]

The King issued a draft declaration regarding religion on September 4. He asked the Presbyterians for their response. Despite all the concessions that it made to the Presbyterians, some were not satisfied. Baxter prepared a Presbyterian reply. Reynolds, supported by Calamy and some others, were troubled by the plainness of Baxter's statement and thought the king would not be pleased. Instead of forcing his declaration upon all the parties, the king summoned seven representatives from the Anglicans and the Presbyterians to his residence, Worcester House, on October 22. It became clear that the Presbyterians were divided between followers of Reynolds and those of Baxter. It was equally clear that the Anglicans did not support the king's policy and they would not grant any concessions to the Presbyterians.

After the breakup of the October 22 meeting, Charles appointed Reynolds, along with Calamy, Morley, and Henchman to put together a revision of the draft declaration. The revised version

2. Jeremiah, *Edward Reynolds*, 246.

of his majesty's "Declaration Concerning Ecclesiastical Affairs," dated October 25, was supported by Gauden and the other moderate Anglicans, but by few others than the Presbyterians. The great issue then became, what was the authority of the royal declaration? The king assumed that he had full authority over religion. Charles declared that since the early days of Christianity the ecclesiastical power was always "subordinate and subject to the civil." This Erastianism, the notion that the civil government had authority over the church, marked all of Charles II's further pronouncements on religion. All deviations allowed by the Declaration of Breda were in accord with the concession to tender consciences offered in the Declaration of Breda. The declaration further referred to the king's obligation to keep his promise, made in the Declaration of Breda, to permit Presbyterians to worship and minister within the Established Church.

The king also promised to convene a group composed of an equal number of Anglican and Presbyterian divine to revise the prayer book. Until that was accomplished, the king gave Presbyterians the right to dispense with any ceremonial practice they found offensive. Specifically, they were exempted from most of the things that the Puritans had objected to, namely kneeling at communion, using the cross in baptism, bowing at the name of Jesus, and wearing the surplus. If the king was able to settle the question of religion, it appeared that the Puritan Presbyterians had won and the High-Church Bishops had lost.

Charles II was generally a man of his word, and also a shrewd politician. He wanted to keep his promises to the Presbyterians, but that required a political solution. Charles proposed one. He would make several of the Presbyterians bishops in the Anglican Church. This would give them a seat and a vote in the House of Lords. The Presbyterians could make common cause with some of the moderate Anglicans.[3] Together they could give strength to the

3. Abernathy, "English Puritans and the Stuart Restoration," 3: "English Presbyterianism varied so much from individual to individual that it defies precise and universal definition . . . In 1640 the position of the English Presbyterians fell, with some exception, between that of the Laudian Anglicans and that of the Scottish Presbyterians."

plan for a modified episcopacy. Also, they would be able to influence the parliamentary elections of 1661. Most importantly, they could support the king's policy among the Presbyterian clergy, and support their continued presence in the Established Church.

On September 9, Reynolds accepted the king's nomination for him to be Bishop of Norwich. Baxter and Calamy were offered the bishoprics of Hereford and Lichfield respectively. Manton, Bates, and Bowles were offered the deanships of Rochester, Lichfield, and York respectively. After some delay they all declined to accept the king's offer. Baxter announced that he preferred to remain a curate in his present parish of Kidderminster. These Presbyterians apparently did not comprehend that they no longer could pick and choose. They became fully supportive of the king, or they could risk losing everything by waiting on the parliament.

As usual for him, Edward Reynolds, DD (now chaplain in ordinary to the king), preached in St. Paul's Church after his appointment as bishop on 1 Cor 6:19–20 "Ye are not your own. For yet are bought with a price: therefore glorify God in your body, and in your spirit, which are God's." Reynolds felt secure enough in his relationship with the king to offer a statement against fornication in his sermon. He stated: "That which alters the end and use for which the body was made, is not to be allowed, but fornication make a quite contrary use of the Body, than that for which it was made, which was to be for the Lord, dedicated to those services wherein he should employ it."[4]

And then Reynolds makes his application in memorable rhetoric: "And God offer Mercy, and I refuse it? Am I bought with a price, and shall I not glorify God by accepting it? I will glorify him in my body; by external purity, and exemplary sanctity. I will let my good works shine before men, that they may glorify God, Mat. 5:16."[5]

Four weeks after his preaching, the Parliament rejected the king's "Declaration Concerning Ecclesiastical Affairs," into which Reynolds had poured his mind and heart. In the end, the other Presbyterians had refused to take the path the king had offered and

4. Jeremiah, *Edward Reynolds*, 261.
5. Jeremiah, *Edward Reynolds*, 262.

Reynolds had accepted. A bishopric meant that they could work with the king to bring about the acceptance of Presbyterianism as a valid part of the Church of England. The other Presbyterians had depended on the parliament for many years, and they did not trust the new king. They could not adjust to the new reality. So, using the old way that had worked for them before, the Presbyterians petitioned to make the "King's Declaration Concerning Ecclesiastical Affairs" into a law of Parliament. Instead, on November 28, by a vote of 183 to 157, the Parliament rejected the king's declaration. The religious settlement was now effectively in the hands of the Parliament.[6]

6. Jeremiah, *Edward Reynolds*, 263.

13

Reynolds Appointed the Bishop of Norwich

WHEN THE CONVENTION PARLIAMENT dissolved itself on December 24, 1660, the only law remaining which protected Presbyterians was the recent "Act for Confirming Ministers in Livings." It was not all-encompassing, and it soon would be undone. By the end of 1660, some 595 ministers, mostly Presbyterians, had been ejected from their livings. Anglicans that had been sequestered during the Interregnum could now displace a Presbyterian or an Independent. Some 290 nonconformists were removed in this manner. This was a harbinger of much worse things to come.

In this religious and political environment, Edward Reynolds was consecrated Bishop of Norwich on January 6, 1661. His seat was the Norwich Cathedral which had served for over four hundred years as a Christian presence in the center of Norfolk. For many centuries, the cathedral was serviced by a Benedictine Monastery whose monks were permitted to talk with visitors in its parlor. The cathedral is a magnificent Gothic structure with an imposing spire that stands out against the English countryside.

Charles II, however, was not done. In another attempt at comprehension, the king convened a new Savoy Conference. Its purpose was to propose revisions in the Book of Common Prayer and to consider alternative forms for the use of Presbyterians. On April 8, 1661, twelve representatives of both Anglicans and

Presbyterians assembled in the Master's Lodging at the Savoy on the Strand, London. The Presbyterians hoped for a discussion that would enable them to understand what the bishops would and would not yield. The bishops, however, said that it was the Presbyterians who wanted the conferences and wanted changes in the prayer book. Therefore, the Presbyterians had to put everything in writing for the bishops to consider.

Only Baxter of the Presbyterians favored this. He thought it would make it possible to allow submitting entirely new forms to the prayer book, which he wanted to do. Reynolds argued that it was not part of the intention of the Presbyterians, since they "admitted the lawfulness of the liturgy and desired information of what they had." Finally, the group acceded to Baxter's wishes. From then on, he worked on his own plan for a whole new liturgy. The rest of the Presbyterians worked on objections to the prayer book which would be presented at a time separate from Baxter's presentation. "Exceptions to the Book of Common Prayer" was drawn up by a group of seven headed by Reynolds. It listed general objections based on "the principle that the liturgy should not be clogged up by things that were doubtful or questioned among pious, learned, and orthodox persons." The Presbyterians hoped that this would lead to a substantive discussion. The Anglicans, however, refused to be drawn into discussion. They stated that the Presbyterians had to prove that the things they listed were unlawful, contrary to the word of God, or of necessity had to be altered.

Baxter's "Reformed Liturgy" was presented the first week in July. The liturgy was primarily one long prayer, longer than the liturgy of the prayer book. The bishops rejected it unanimously. Finally, after four months, the bishops were willing to debate the items to which the Presbyterians objected. Only Baxter, among the Presbyterians, had a furious eagerness to engage in a dispute. Two Presbyterians joined with him and debated three Anglicans beginning on July 23, 1661.

The conference ended in complete failure. The only report agreed upon by both sides was a statement that "all were agreed on the ends of the church's welfare, unity and peace and his majesty's happiness and contentment, but that all their debates, would dis-agree in the means." Baxter drew up an "Account of our Endeavors" to be presented to the King. Representatives of the court indicated that the report would be accepted only if Reynolds and some others accompanied Baxter. When they did so, Reynolds made a brief address, and Manton delivered the petition to the king, which he graciously accepted. Nothing came of it.

There was yet another body with authority over ecclesiastical matters—the Provincial Convocation which had been held in each area over the last four hundred years. Along with the Archbishops of Canterbury and York, the convocation was made up of the bishops and two clergy from each district. The clergy formed a lower house and the bishops formed the upper house. These convocations made decisions and implemented changes in the worship and life of the church. When the convocation met in November 1661, a committee of eight bishops was appointed to finalize revisions to the Book of Common Prayer. Bishops Cosin and Wren were the primary authors. Although they were disciples of the late Archbishop Laud, Laudian influence was "barely apparent" in this revision. The moderates, including Reynolds, seemed to win a modest victory. The Presbyterians' "Exceptions to the Book of Common Prayer" from the Savoy Conference had considerable influence.

In the final days of the convocation, Reynolds was the personal mover of two major additions to the prayer book. His patient and modest work at the Savoy Conference, and before, created an openness by the other bishops to his offerings. It is widely known that Reynolds was the author of the "General Thanksgiving," which continues to be used for morning prayer, and sometimes evening prayer, during weekday services. Some have noted a similarity of Reynolds's prayer with the "Prayer of Thanksgiving or Blessing of the Bread and Wine" in the Westminster Assembly's Directory for the Public Worship of God.

This prayer is as follows:

> Almighty God, Father of all mercies, we thine unworthy
> servants do give thee most humble and hearty thanks for
> all they goodness and loving kindness to us and to all men

[sic]; (particularly to those who desire now to offer up their praises and thanksgivings for late mercies vouchsafed unto them). We bless thee for our creation, preservation, and all the blessings of this life, but above for thine inestimable love in the redemption of the world by our Lord Jesus Christ; for the means of grace, and for the hope of glory. And we beseech thee give us that due sense of all thy mercies, that our hearts may be unfeignedly thankful, and we shew thy praise, and by walking before thee in holiness and righteousness all our days, through Jesus Christ our Lord, to whom with thee and the holy Ghost be all honor and glory, world without end.[1]

Another prayer, a collect for "All Conditions of Men," also appears to have been written by Reynolds. It follows:

O God, the creator and preserver of all mankind, we humbly beseech thee for all sorts and conditions of men, that thou wouldst be pleased to make they ways known unto them, thy saving health unto all nations. More especially we pray for the good estate of the Catholic Church, that it may be so guided and governed by thy good Spirit, that all who profess and call themselves Christians may be led into the way of truth, and hold the faith in unity of spirit, in the bond of peace, and in righteousness of life. Finally we commend to thy fatherly goodness all those who are in any way afflicted, or distressed in mind, body, or estate (especially those for whom our prayers are desired), that it may please thee to comfort and relieve them according to their several necessities, giving them patience under their sufferings, and a happy issue out of their afflictions. And this we beg for Jesus Christ his sake. Amen.[2]

1. See the "Prayer of Humble Access" in Episcopal Church, *Book of Common Prayer*, 362.

2. Reynolds rarely makes any reference to people or activities in New England. The principal reason is that Presbyterians as a group were not immigrating to the New World. Until 1662, and the Act of Uniformity, they had reason to believe that they were going to accomplish their goals in England.

Puritans had long wanted to modify the prayer book. Edward Reynolds, as Bishop of Norwich, introduced eighteen changes recommended by Puritan Presbyterians, the majority of which were accepted.

14

Norwich's Bishop, Pride of the Presbyterians

A Calvinist in Anglican Clothing

BEING BISHOP OF NORWICH was not an easy role for Edward Reynolds. Better said, Reynolds had to take up the task of reinstituting Episcopal order in a diocese where it had been out of favor for nearly six decades.[1] On the one hand, Reynolds should have felt at home because Norwich had a tradition of Puritanism dating from the reign of Queen Elizabeth. The local attitudes were augmented by the immigration of cloth-workers, Dutch and Flemish, who began to come to Norwich in the 1570s and continued into the seventeenth century. They were mostly Protestants whose faith had been tested by Roman Catholic persecution and who were supportive of church life similar to Puritanism.

Attempts by previous bishops to enforce Laudianism had been resisted. The three Laudian bishops prior to Reynolds had created widespread resentment against the established church.

1. Jeremiah, "Edward Reynolds," 317. The diocese of Norwich, which included the counties of Norfolk, Suffolk, and part of Cambridgeshire in the seventeenth century, had been a stronghold of Puritanism since early in Queen Elizabeth's reign.

The first, and worst, was Matthew Wren (1635–38), an extremely zealous follower of Archbishop Laud. So great was the hostility towards his demands for conformity that a large number of Puritan tradesman emigrated to Norfolk, either to the continent, or to the American colonies. In fact, a large number of the tradesmen had emigrated from Norwich. So those who remained should have welcomed Reynolds, who represented a form of Puritanism—even though they might have never heard of Presbyterianism. In this setting, the appointment of Reynolds to the see of Norwich was a wise move on the part of the king.

Reynolds worked diligently at the task of restoring trust in the established church by encouraging moderation and comprehension within the diocese.[2] By staying true to his own principles of focusing on essentials and allowing latitude on nonessentials, he encouraged many diocesan ministers to conform. In Norwich, under Reynolds, conformity meant adherence to the essentials of the Christian faith, rather than strict compliance with all the details of the church Anglican settlement. [3]

The Laudian bishops resented Reynolds's refusal to enforce all of the High-Church practices—moving the communion table against the east wall, fencing it off from the people, requiring kneeling for the communion, using the sign of the cross at baptism, and wearing the surplice by clergy. However, they could not interfere with Reynolds's governance in his own diocese. Reynolds instituted his policy of comprehension before the Act of Uniformity in 1662 and maintained it afterward until his death.

Reynolds made clear his policy and his pastoral heart early in his service in Norwich in a sermon entitled "Preaching of Christ" at St. Peter's Church in the City of Norwich at an ordination on September 22, 1661. The text was 2 Corinthians 4:5: "For we do not proclaim ourselves; we proclaim Jesus Christ as Lord,

2. "Comprehension," which Reynolds desired, was the concept that there was to be one uniform religion, sanctioned and enforced by the state. Even from the time of Henry VIII through the early years of Reynolds's ministry, it assumed an episcopal form and a generally Reformed or Calvinist theology.

3. Jeremiah, "Edward Reynolds," 378. "Reynolds also believed that as a Bishop he would enjoy the freedom to rule in his diocese as he saw fit."

and ourselves as your slaves for Jesus sake." In the dedication of the sermon (published in 1662), Reynolds's address was "To the Reverend my dearly beloved Brethren the Dean, Prebendaries, and the rest of the Clergy of the Cathedral Church and the City of Norwich." His first point was "That I might provoke my younger brethren to make it the main degree of their ministry to render the Lord Jesus . . . [and not] the conceptions of their own heart, rather than his counsel." Second was his desire to be only first among equals with his clergy.[4] He promised to consult them "in matters of weight and difficulty." He felt that this would lead to "The more safe, judicious, regular, and inoffensive determining of them." He concluded by calling himself, "Your most loving Brother and fellow laborer in the service of Christ and His Church."[5]

In the sermon, Reynolds returns to one of his most familiar themes, namely, the necessity of a learned ministry. He declared that preaching was "not the work of an illiterate reader, but one who hath both the tongue of the learned, a workman that need not be ashamed. This is not the work of a careless loiterer that shears the fleece and starves the flock but one who gives himself wholly to it." This critique was certainly directed, not only at the sectarians, but also at some ministers in this diocese who did not preach themselves but had someone read a lesson during the service.[6]

Reynolds described three qualifications for "so weighty a work as preaching": (1) sanctity of life, an inner godliness; (2) soundness of orthodox doctrine; (3) an aptness to teach. His strong support for a learned ministry, displaying these three qualities that he recommended, was in contrast to what he felt prevailed in the recent past. In the "late licentious days amongst us . . . men made it the principal business of their usurped preaching in disgrace and pull down legitimate preachers."[7]

---

4. Jeremiah, "Edward Reynolds," 320. "Reynolds understood his office in a gradus rather than an ordu sense. The gradus Bishop saw himself as a president of Presbyters in its diocese as opposed to a lord over inferior clergy."

5. Jeremiah, *Edward Reynolds*, 321.

6. Jeremiah, *Edward Reynolds*, 322.

7. Jeremiah, *Edward Reynolds*, 323.

Reynolds not only made his principles clear by speaking about them, but he also applied them in the necessary work of a bishop in his visitation to the parishes of his diocese. All of the bishops of the Church of England were given a set of visitation articles which they were expected to follow. Naturally, they were applied variously by each bishop. The standard articles were asked if the king's supremacy was preached four times a year, and if any false, heretical, dangerous, or seditious doctrine was preached. For some of the Laudian inclined bishops, Presbyterian doctrine might be counted in the unacceptable category.

Reynolds asked if the parish minister preached "only sound doctrine, tending to peace, holiness and edification, consonant with the Word of God, and the doctrine contained in the Church of England?" Further, Reynolds was concerned whether the minister preached "constantly" in the church. For some bishops, having some officially sanctioned homily read was sufficient. For Reynolds, preaching of biblical texts was necessary. If the parish minister could not do it, then he should arrange for another minister to do it in his place.

Having made his principles clear to the clergy of his diocese both in speech and action, Reynolds chose an invitation to preach to the magistrates and members of the corporation at Yarmouth in Norfolk as an occasion to make his policy clear to the public of his diocese. The sermon was entitled "Staves of Beauty and Bands." It was preached on August 23, 1661 on the text of Zechariah 11:7: "I took unto me Two Staves; the one I call Beauty, and the other I called Bands, and I fed the Flock." Reynolds used these two names to refer to the two noble ends of the pastoral office. They represented for him "the Restoring of Beauty to his Church corrupted, and a Unity to his Church divided. Beauty referred to Christ's Word, Ordinances, and Government, being as glorious things in themselves."[8] Bands referred to unity. As a man was created by the hand of God there was an exact harmony and agreement among his faculties: "his Affections consonant unto his Will, His Will to

---

8. Jeremiah, *Edward Reynolds*, 323.

his Reason, and his Reason to God."[9] There is a moral unity in the church. It is the unity of faith, obedience, worship, ends, and designs. But beyond all these and most important is the bond of unity in the communion of Christ's Spirit.[10]

Reynolds was doing his best to present an Episcopal Church that was centered in Christ and willing to be flexible in nonessentials. Soon the House of Commons acted to make life more difficult for any nonconformists to strict High-Church Anglicanism. In 1664, the Cavalier Parliament passed the Conventicle Act, which prohibited all nonconformist religious gatherings of more than five persons. As if in response to extremist severity, beginning in 1664 a series of great calamities fell upon England which caused many people to fear that God was angry and judging the nation. In late 1664, a flea-borne bubonic plague struck London. By the following summer, three thousand people a week were dying. The plague peaked at more than seven thousand deaths a week in mid-September of 1665. Everyone who could leave the city did so, including the king.

The city had not yet recovered fully from the plague when, in 1666, the Great Fire of London nearly reduced the city to ashes. This time Charles stayed in the city. He directed relief efforts and even worked side by side with commoners, handling buckets of water. Later the defeat of the Royal Navy by the Dutch at Medway in June 1667 increased the general sense of discouragement. In the midst of all these tragedies, the fear of emergent popery rose again.

For Reynolds, God's hand was in all things. If the events were harmful to Christians, God meant them to lead to repentance. If they were helpful, God meant them to encourage righteousness and holiness of life. Reynolds preached to the peers in the Abby Church at Westminster on November 7, 1666. It was a day of solemn humiliation "for the continuing Pestilence." Reynolds left no

9. Jeremiah, *Edward Reynolds*, 324.

10. Jeremiah, *Edward Reynolds*, 384. "The posthumous publication of Reynolds' sermon and treatises show that the influence of his thought extended into the devotional, doctrinal and political areas of English life from the seventeenth to the nineteenth centuries."

doubt as to his interpretation of the events of the last two years. The Lord had shown great mercy in the return of Charles II to the throne without bloodshed. A way was open for a durable settlement of church and state. But because the people of England had not responded to these mercies with a comprehensive and moderate church settlement, God was angry.

Did the people repent and reform? No. So God's anger was undiminished. "He hath likewise contended by Fire, and by the late direful conflagration, that laid in Ashes the glorious Metropolis of this Nation, hath made desolate almost all her goodly Palaces, and laid waste almost all the Sanctuaries of God therein."[11] The proper response to God's anger was contained in the text that Reynolds chose to expound. It was Philippians 4:5: "Let your Moderation be known among all Men. The Lord is at hand."[12] Some predicted that when Reynolds entered his calling as Bishop of Norwich, he would withdraw from activity on the national scene. Quite the opposite was the case. In this sermon to the House of Lords, Reynolds laid the groundwork for his advocacy of several bills before the Parliament that would make the religious settlement broad and more inclusive. Moderation was the key principle. That principle applied to people's individual lives and also to the policies of the state.

The fact that the Lord is at hand was both a comfort and a challenge. Reynolds brought his theology of grace and judgment together in response to the English situation. "Thus let your Moderation be known to all men, because the Lord is at hand in his future approaching judgments . . . as if he would both ways try, whether by the one we would be led unto Repentance, or by the other learn Righteousness."[13]

Reynolds' sermon met with much praise. It was printed in two editions in 1666. It seemed that Reynolds's sermon would bear fruit. A number of powerful laymembers of Parliament with some bishops prepared a comprehension bill for the fall of 1667. This time the king, major court officials, and eight bishops were

11. Jeremiah, *Edward Reynolds*, 329.
12. Jeremiah, *Edward Reynolds*, 330.
13. Jeremiah, *Edward Reynolds*, 331.

involved. Reynolds was one of the bishops. The leader of the effort was John Wilkins, a leader in the scientific community during restoration. His views were similar to Reynolds. The strategy was to keep the plan quiet and then present it to the House of Commons before the High Church party could prepare a counterattack.

Wilkins made a major error in judgment. He shared it with his good friend Seth Ward, Bishop of Salisbury. Ward furnished the plan to the opposition, who then prepared a massive attack on it. Even though the king spoke in favor of the bill, it was overwhelmingly defeated. The vengeful bishops and the younger radical Royalists in the Cavalier Parliament were proudly defiant of both the king and the nation.

Reynolds took the opportunity of preaching before the king on Easter Day, March 22, 1667, to respond to the defeat at comprehension. Reynolds expounded on the text of Hebrews 13:20–21: "Now the God of Peace, that brought again from the Dead our Lord Jesus Christ, that great Shepherd of the Sheep, through the blood of the Everlasting Covenant, Make you perfect in every Good Work to do his will, working in you that which is well pleasing in his sight, through Jesus Christ."[14] He immediately applied it to his hearers. "Now because the sum of our Happiness here stands in two things, That God is at peace with us, and that we live in obedience to him. He could not avoid making the contrast between what ought to be, and what was at present. How should All whom the God of Peace hath entrusted with the care of his House . . . put forth their utmost and most zealous Endeavors to close up these doleful Breaches which are among us."[15] Reynolds was convinced that a more moderate church settlement would not only bring in more Protestant nonconformists, but it would also strengthen the church, spiritually revive the nation, and be a strong bulwark against potential encroachments of Roman Catholicism. So Reynolds again brought the issue before the king.

On the 28th of March, 1669, Reynolds preached before King Charles II. His text was Philippians 3:8: "Yea doubtless, and I count

14. Jeremiah, *Edward Reynolds*, 335.
15. Jeremiah, *Edward Reynolds*, 336.

all things but loss for the excellency of the Knowledge of Christ Jesus my Lord."[16] The sermon was biblical and evangelical. It was certainly designed to bring the king to repentance of his sin, and salvation in Christ. In summation Reynolds proclaimed: "Thus we see the absolute necessity of the Gospel, wherein we find Christ meritoriously purchasing, God graciously conveying, Repentance humbly disposing, Faith comfortably receiving, and sincere obedience gradually conducting us unto eternal salvation." And he finished by stating, "And here I cannot but with grief of heart once more bewail those divisions which endanger the beauty, and shake the stability of this once flourishing Church."

Edward Reynolds did not confine his ecclesiastical activities only to preaching. Charles II and the church had set a clerical "poverty line" of fifty pounds per year. The incomes provided by many of the parishes did not even come up to that line. Reynolds provided 268 pounds per year to a group of fourteen vicarages in his diocese. He actively helped his clergy financially in other ways as well. He was praised as a great benefactor of poor widows and the children of deceased clergymen. At one point he personally lent the city of Norwich two hundred pounds for the poor. He even gave 440 pounds for the rebuilding of St. Paul's Cathedral in London, which had been burned in the Great Fire.

Where he could, Reynolds brought members of his family into a relationship as colleagues in ministry. His namesake, Edward, graduated from Magdalen College, Oxford and was ordained as vicar of St. Peter's Northampton. When the archdeacon of Norfolk died on January 15, 1661, his father, as the newly installed Bishop of Norwich, appointed his son, Edward, as archdeacon. Finally, and most notably, Reynolds ordained his son-in-law, John Conant, on September 18, 1670 and he served as vicar of All Saints, Northampton from 1679–89.[17]

Reynolds's health began to fail in 1669. The kidney stones which had plagued him on and off for years now brought constant pain. His gastrointestinal system balked at proper elimination

16. Jeremiah, *Edward Reynolds*, 342.

17. Jeremiah, *Edward Reynolds*, 343.

and physicians at the time had no clear vision of how to treat it. Reynolds restricted his public activities. However, contrary to his wishes, Reynolds was obliged to host a royal visit to Norwich in 1671. His wife, Mary, took the primary responsibility and saw to it that King Charles II, his Queen Catherine, the Duke of York, the Duke of Monmouth, the Duke of Buckingham, and all their entourage were properly housed in Norwich and properly feted at the bishop's palace. Reynolds could not escape all the pomp and ceremony that went with his office, which was not only religious, but also highly political.[18]

Edward Reynolds, Lord Bishop of Norwich, died on July 28, 1676, a century before the American Revolution, which he could never have envisioned. He was buried in a vault in the chapel he had built next to the cathedral. Twenty-first-century Americans have barely heard of him. Current Anglicans in the places he had frequented, Oxford, London, and Norwich, know him only as the author of the weekday "Morning Prayer of Thanksgiving" in the Book of Common Worship. He would have been glad to be so remembered.

Benedict Rively preached the funeral sermon for Edward Reynolds. Rively stated that Reynolds was "a good man . . . a good Christian . . . a good minister of the gospel . . . and a good Bishop."[19] What could not be doubted was that Reynolds had lived a blameless life, free from scandal. He possessed, in Rively's words, "a grave, venerable aspect and behavior." He had served as "a veteran soldier in the faith of Christ." As the "ecclesiastical governor" of the diocese, the results of Reynolds's "wise and good government" were such that in no other diocese could there be found "a more sober, regular, and loyal clergy, a more comfortable people, more decent and well repaired churches. And a greater alteration both of the judgments and manners of men." Daniel Neal wrote of Reynolds, "He was reckoned one of the most eloquent men of his age, and a good old Puritan."

18. Jeremiah, *Edward Reynolds*, 344.

19. Jeremiah, *Edward Reynolds*, 316.

Edward Reynolds was, indeed, the pride of the Presbyterian Party in seventeenth-century England. Further, he was a worthy Calvinist in Anglican Clothing.

Postscript

AN INTERESTING FINAL COMMENT was found in the notes of late Reynolds scholar Jack B. Rogers.[1] He wrote:

> Edward Reynolds was the final Puritan. He continued to adhere to all of the early Puritan Presbyterian values . . . He continued to honor the Monarch. He continued to work for reformation within the Church of England in a Calvinist manner theologically and a Presbyterian manner governmentally. He continued to make the authority of the Bible the foundation of his ministry. And he continued to live a life of simple piety in his family, and with moderation in the affairs of the church.

Rogers was a former colleague of H. Newton Malony, senior author of this manuscript, at Fuller Theological Seminary. He became, in retirement, a research scholar at Huntington Memorial Library in San Marino, California. His special interest was in Edward Reynolds and the development of Presbyterian theological history. He served for a term as stated clerk for the Presbyterian Church USA. After Rogers's untimely death, Malony agreed to undertake publication of Rogers's research investigations.

---

1. Rogers. *Presbyterian Creeds*, 67. Roger was a student of the legacy of Edward Reynolds. As the former Moderator of the Presbyterian Church USA, he knows well the differences between contemporary USA conception of 'Puritans' and the reality of the Mayflower settlers. This was a personal note not previously published.

Concerning Reynolds's many publications, it was unusual to have a volume of someone's "works" published during that person's lifetime. However , Edward Reynolds's *Works* was first published in 1658. Another edition was published in 1679, soon after his death. The year after Reynolds's death, his son, Edward, edited and published yet another sermon of his father's, *Meditations on the Fall and Rising of St. Peter.* In the early nineteenth century there was a brief revival of interest in Reynolds. *The Whole Works of the Right Reverend Edward Reynolds, D.D. Lord Bishop of Norwich* were published in six volumes. Volume 1 begins with fifty-six pages of memoirs of the life of the author by Alexander Chalmers. Also, an explication of the 110th Psalm, originally published in 1632, was also published separately in the nineteenth century.

Edward Reynolds's earliest work, *A Treatise of the Passions and Faculties of the Soule of Man: with the Several Dignities and Corruptions Thereunto Belonging* was first published, at the request of Elizabeth Princess Palatine in 1640 in two slightly different editions. Another edition was published in 1651. A third edition (with a portrait of the author inscribed in the front piece) appeared in 1656. A fourth edition was published in 1658. The most recent publication of this treatise was *An Old but Very Modern Manual of Mental Health* by Edward Reynolds in 1640; an edited version for modern readers was published by Jack B. Rogers and H. Newton Malony, in 2019.

Fortunately for Malony, Rogers had discovered that Jeffrey J. Jeremiah had written a major doctoral dissertation at George Washington University in 1992 on Edward Reynolds's (1599–1676) "Pride of the Presbyterian Party." This encyclopedic text became the foundation for the present publication. Significantly, Jeremiah joins Malony as co-author in this volume. Jeremiah serves as the clerk of the Evangelical Presbyterian Church.

Bibliography

Abernathy, George R., Jr. "The English Puritans and the Stuart Restoration, 1648–1663." *Transactions of the American Philosophical Society* 55.2 (1965) 3–10.

Ackroyd, Peter. *Rebellion: The History of England from James I to the Glorious Revolution.* New York: St Martin's Press, 2014.

Arnold, Catherine. *City of Sin: London and its Vices.* London: Simon and Schuster, 2010.

Benedict, Alexander Chalmers, and Riveley Edward Reynolds, eds. *The Whole Works of the Right Rev. Edward Reynolds, Lord Bishop of Norwich.* New York: Google Books, 1826.

Braddick, Michael, ed. *The Oxford Handbook of the English Revolution.* Oxford: Oxford University Press, 2015.

Carter, C. Sydney. "Edward Reynolds (1599–1675): A Puritan Bishop." *Churchman* 58.2 (1944) 1–5.

Chapiro, Lisa, ed. and trans. *The Correspondence between Princess Elizabeth of Bohemia and René Descartes.* Chicago: University of Chicago Press, 2007.

Cressy, David. *Charles I and the People of England.* Oxford: Oxford University Press, 2015.

Cummings, Brian, ed. *Book of Common Prayer: Texts of 1549, 1559, and 1662.* Oxford: Oxford University Press, 2011.

"Declaration of Breda." https://en.wikipedia.org/wiki/Declaration_of_Breda.

Descartes, René. *Discourse on the Method of Rightly Conducting One's Reason and Seeking Truth in the Sciences.* Leiden: Maire, 1637.

———. *Principles of Philosophy.* Translated by Valentine Miller and Reese P. Miller. Dordrecht, The Netherlands: Reidel, 1983.

———. *Treatise of Man.* Translation and commentary by Thomas Steele Hall. Cambridge: Harvard University Press, 1972.

Donagan, Barbara. "Did Ministers Matter? War and Religion in England, 1642–1649." *The Journal of British Studies* 33 (1994) 119–56.

———. "Puritan Ministers and Laymen: Professional Claims and Social Constraints in Seventeenth Century England." *Huntington Library Quarterly* 47 (1984) 91–111.

Bibliography

"Edward Reynolds." https://en.wikipedia.org/wiki/Edward_Reynolds.

The Episcopal Church. *The Book of Common Prayer : and Administration of the Sacraments and Other Rites and Ceremonies of the Church, according to the Use of the Protestant Episcopal Church in the United States of America : Together with the Psalter or Psalms of David.* New York: Seabury, 1953.

"Evangelical Presbyterian Church." https://en.wikipedia.org/wiki/Evangelical_Presbyterian_Church_(United_States).

Evans, J. T. *Seventeenth-Century Norwich: Politics, Religion, and Government, 1620–690.* Oxford: Clarendon, 1979.

Hall, Basil. "Puritanism: the Problem of Definition." In *Studies in Church Histry, Volume II,* edited by G. J. Cuming, 283–96. London: Nelson, 1965.

"History of the Puritans from 1649." https://en.wikipedia.org/wiki/History_of_the_Puritans_from_1649.

Jeremiah, Jeffrey Jon. "Edward Reynolds (1599–1676): 'Pride of the Presbyterian Party.'" PhD diss., George Washington University, Washington DC, 1992.

Kelly, Douglas F. *The Westminster Shorter Catechism in Modern English.* Phillipsburg: Presbyterian and Reformed, 1986.

"King James I." https://en.wikipedia.org/wiki/James_VI_and_I.

"King James Version." https://en.wikipedia.org/wiki/King_James_Version.

Latourette, Kenneth Scott. *A History of Christianity.* Vol. 2, *The Reformation to the Present.* Peabody: Prince, 1997.

Masson, David. *The Life of John Milton: Narrated in Connexion with the Political, Ecclesiastical, and Literary History of His Time.* Vol. 5, *1654–1660.* London: Macmillan and Co., 1877.

McCullough, Peter, et al., eds. *The Oxford Handbook of the Early Modern Sermon.* Oxford: Oxford University Press, 2011.

McKim, Donald K. *The Westminster Handbook of Reformed Theology.* Louisville: John Knox, 2001.

"Old Jewry." https://en.wikipedia.org/wiki/Old_Jewry.

Paul, Robert S. *The Assembly of the Lord: Politics and Religion in the Westminster Assembly and the "Grand Debate."* Edinburgh: T. & T. Clark, 1985.

Philbrick, Nathaniel. *Mayflower: A Story of Courage, Community, and War.* New York: Viking, 2006.

Pitman, John Rogers. *The Whole Works of the Right Rev. Edward Reynolds, D.D. Lord Bishop of Norwich; Now First Collected, With His Funeral Sermon, by B. Riveley, One of His Lordship's Chaplains. To Which Is Prefixed a Memoir of the Life of the Author, by Alexander Chalmers, F.S.A.* 6 vols. London: Holdsworth, 1826.

Reynolds, Edward. *Divers Sermons Preached on Several Occasions.* London: Printed by Tho. Ratcliffe for George Thomason at the Sign of the Rose and Crown in St Paul's Church-yard, 1659.

———. *An Old but Very Modern Manual of Mental Health.* Edited by Jack R. Rogers and H. Newton Malony. Bloomington: Ketch, 2019.

———. *A Treatise of the Passions and Faculties of the Soul of Man, With the Several Dignities and Corruptions thereunto Belonging.* London: Bostock, 1640.

Bibliography

————. *The Whole Works of the Right Reverend Edward Reynolds, D.D. Lord Bishop of Norwich.* 6 vols. London: Holdsworth, 1826.

————. *The Works of the Right Reverend in God, Edward Reynolds, D.D.: Late Lord Bishop of Norwich. Containing Three Treatises of the Vanity of the Creature. The Sinfulness of Sin. Life of Christ. An Explication of Psalm CX. Meditations on the Sacrament of the Lord's Supper. An Explication of the XIV. Chapter of Hosea. A Treatise of the Passions and Faculties of the Soul. With a Collection of Thirty Sermons Preached on Several Solemn Occasions.* 6 vols. London: Printed by Tho Newcomb, and are to be sold by Robert Boulter at the Turks-Head in Cornhill, over against the Royal Exchange, 1679.

Reynolds, Edward. *Meditations on the Fall and Rising of St. Peter.* London: Parkurst, 1677.

Robertson, Geoffrey. *The Tyrannicide Brief: The Story of the Man Who Sent Charles I to the Scafford.* New York: Pantheon, 2005.

Rogers, Jack Bartlett. *Presbyterian Creeds: A Guide to the Book of Confessions.* Louisville: Westminster John Knox, 1985.

————. *Scripture in the Westminster: A Problem of Historical Interpretation for American Presbyterians.* Grand Rapids: Eerdmans, 1967.

Rogers, Jack B., and Forrest E. Baird. *Introduction to Philosophy: A Case Method Approach.* San Francisco: Harper & Row, 1981.

Seaver, Paul S. *The Puritan Lectureships: The Politics of Religious Dissent, 1560–562.* Stanford: Stanford University Press, 1970.

Shapiro, Lisa, ed. and trans. *The Correspondence between Princess Elisabeth of Bohemia and Rene Descartes.* Chicago: The University of Chicago Press, 2007.

Spurr, John. *English Puritanism: 1603–1689.* New York: St. Martin's, 1998.

Toon, Peter, ed. *The Correspondence of John Owen (1616–1683).* Cambridge: Clarke, 1970.

Uglow, Jenny. *A Gambling Man: Charles II's Restoration Game.* New York: Farrar, Straus & Giroux, 2009.

Van Dixhoorn, Chad B. *Reforming the Reformation: Theological Debate at the Westminister Assembly 1643–1652.* 7 vols. PhD diss., Cambridge, Cambridge University, 2005.

Webster, Tom. *Godly Clergy in Early Stuart England: The Caroline Puritan Movement c.1560–643.* Cambridge: Cambridge University Press, 1997.

Whitaker, Katie. *A Royal Passion: The Turbulent Marriage of King Charles I of England and Henrietta Maria of France.* New York: Norton, 2010.

"William Laud." https://en.wikipedia.org/wiki/William_Laud.

Williamson, G. I. *The Westminster Confession of Faith for Study Classes.* 2nd ed. Phillipsburg: Presbyterian and Reformed, 1979.

————. *The Westminster Shorter Catechism.* Phillipsburg: Presbyterian and Reformed, 2005.

Wilson, Jim. *900 Years: Norwich Cathedral and Diocese.* Norwich, England: Jurvold, 1996.